T0323903

Cambridge Elements ☰

Elements in Publishing and Book Culture
edited by
Samantha J. Rayner
University College London
Leah Tether
University of Bristol

UNPRINTED
Publication Beyond the Press

Daria Kohler, *KU Leuven*

Daniel Wakelin, *University of Oxford*

Natascha Domeisen, *Domeisen Rare Books*

Daniel Haywood, *University of Oxford*

Edward Jones, *British School at Athens*

Micah Mackay, *University of Oxford*

Rosie Maxton, *University of Oxford*

Brian M. Moore, *University of Oxford*

Katie Noble, *University of Oxford*

Felix M. Simon, *University of Oxford*

Daniel Wojahn, *University of Oxford*

CAMBRIDGE
UNIVERSITY PRESS

Shaftesbury Road, Cambridge CB2 8EA, United Kingdom

One Liberty Plaza, 20th Floor, New York, NY 10006, USA

477 Williamstown Road, Port Melbourne, VIC 3207, Australia

314–321, 3rd Floor, Plot 3, Splendor Forum, Jasola District Centre,
New Delhi – 110025, India

103 Penang Road, #05–06/07, Visioncrest Commercial, Singapore 238467

Cambridge University Press is part of Cambridge University Press & Assessment,
a department of the University of Cambridge.

We share the University's mission to contribute to society through the pursuit of
education, learning and research at the highest international levels of excellence.

www.cambridge.org
Information on this title: www.cambridge.org/9781009545310

DOI: 10.1017/9781009545327

When citing this work, please include a reference to the DOI 10.1017/9781009545327

First published 2025

A catalogue record for this publication is available from the British Library

ISBN 978-1-009-54531-0 Paperback
ISSN 2514-8524 (online)
ISSN 2514-8516 (print)

Unprinted

Publication Beyond the Press

Elements in Publishing and Book Culture

DOI: 10.1017/9781009545327
First published online: January 2025

Daria Kohler and Daniel Wakelin *et al.*

Author for correspondence: Daria Kohler, daria.kohler@kuleuven.be

ABSTRACT: This Element explores the idea of publication in media used before, alongside, and after print. It contrasts multiple traditions of unprinted communication in their diversity and particularity. This decentres print as the means for understanding publication; instead, *publication* is seen as an heuristic term that identifies activities these traditions share, but that also differ in ways not reducible to comparisons with printing. The Element engages with texts written on papyrus, chiselled in stone, and created digitally; sung, proclaimed, and put on stage; banned, hidden, and rediscovered. The authors move between Greek inscriptions and Tibetan edicts, early modern manuscripts and AI-assisted composition, monasteries and courts, constantly questioning the term *publication* and considering the agency of people publishing and the publics they address. The picture that transpires is that of a colourful variety of contexts of production and dissemination, underlining the value of studying 'unprinted' publication in its own right.

This Element also has a video abstract: www.cambridge.org/unprinted-abstract

KEYWORDS: book history, publication, circulation of texts, performance, materiality of text

ISBNs: 9781009545310 (PB), 9781009545327 (OC)
ISSNs: 2514-8524 (online), 2514-8516 (print)

Contents

Foreword

The UK's Leverhulme Trust sponsored fifteen scholarships for doctoral students at the University of Oxford between 2018 and 2023. Each student in this Leverhulme Doctoral Centre explored some aspect of the theme 'publication beyond print' in an area of the humanities or social sciences. This Element presents some of their research in short sections, each focused on a particular discipline, but building on each other in turn. Beyond brief introductions, each contribution is discreet and has a single author, but the contributions were composed after discussion and planning as a group and were reviewed by all the authors as a whole. This book thus, though short, has multiple authors – a miniature multigraph. It takes some inspiration from the Multigraph Collective's *Interacting with Print: Elements of Reading in the Era of Print Saturation* (2018), which presents 'a new kind of scholarly object' that 'exceeds the normal scale of scriptural collaboration'.[1] Its shared authorship and its circulation largely online are experiments in 'publication beyond the press' that the book considers.

---

[1] The Multigraph Collective, *Interacting with Print: Elements of Reading in the Era of Print Saturation* (Chicago: University of Chicago Press, 2018), xi.

1 What Are Publication and the Press?

We aim to sidestep the dominance of the printed word in the study of human culture and society by examining other media used before, alongside, and after print. We aim to question the assumptions that self-expression, political community, and intellectual progress are best forged by printing. To do so, we range across unprinted media from inscriptions, handwriting, speech, and song into typewriting and AI-assisted composition. Through detailed examples, we consider how methods of publication work beyond the press.

Our book is not primarily about emergent new media – they are just one phenomenon among many, upsetting the focus on the present in many discussions of publication – we look more widely across 2,500 years of history and two continents in geography. But one of our hopes is that thinking about past modes of publication can help us to think about future ones. And the time is ripe to explore communication in media other than print. In the twenty-first century, print competes with digital communication; political movements start on social media; novels are often read on screen; and digital formats allow would-be writers to self-publish more readily.[2] In light of these new perspectives, and as we remember the long history of speech, handwriting, and carving, print publication looks like a mere interlude or local curiosity – in one historical model, a 'Gutenberg Parenthesis'. In this phrase, popularized by Jeff Jarvis, digital communication in the future will be 'a mirror image' of handwritten communication in the past, operating 'symmetrically'.[3] We do not think that the correlations are so neat, for the particularity and diversity of the examples in our book reveal no single or simple image to be the 'mirror' of digital media. But the transformation from printed to digital publishing – in news, book publishing, and self-promotion on social media – does help us to recognize that

[2] N. S. Baron, *Words Onscreen* (Oxford: Oxford University Press, 2015);
A. Phillips, *Turning the Page: The Evolution of the Book* (London: Routledge, 2014), 120–3.
[3] J. Jarvis, *The Gutenberg Parenthesis* (New York: Bloomsbury, 2023), 5, 13.

particularity and diversity without measuring acts of publication only by their likeness to print.

The connection between printing and publishing was never exclusive, for the press has not been limited to what is conventionally considered publication. It was also used for jobbing printing (from the earliest moments, in 'pardons' made by Johann Gutenberg or William Caxton themselves), lined notepaper, and forms to fill in, the unliterary productions of all sorts of ephemera.[4] Conversely, there was a variety of modes of publishing in other media even *alongside* print, during that so-called Parenthesis, as manuscript scholars have long shown.[5] After all, some countries, subcultures, or traditions only adopted the press several centuries after it became predominant for book publication in western Europe – even in neighbouring Iceland or the Ottoman empire, for example (as in one of our case studies). And even where books tended to be printed, other kinds of texts continued to circulate unprinted, sometimes in relation to print but complementing or contrasting it (as in other case studies on German manuscripts or English theatre). So we look at publishing beyond the press: before it, alongside it, and after it.

The question is whether, and if so how, the ways of sharing texts examined here can be considered as publishing. Is it an anachronistic term? Its suitability for unprinted communication has been questioned most carefully by medievalists: Samu Niskanen, who does adopt the term, has noted that other medievalists avoided calling the circulation of texts in manuscript *publication*, implicitly judging the term inappropriate. He suggested that for many 'the idea of publication is so thoroughly associated with the rapid multiplication of copies by the printing press, it is perceived as foreign to the realities of the circulation of books in

---

[4] For the examples, see P. Needham, *The Printer and the Pardoner* (Washington, DC: Library of Congress, 1986); L. Gitelman, *Paper Knowledge: Toward a Media History of Documents* (Durham, NC: Duke University Press, 2014); K. D. Murphy and S. O'Driscoll, eds., *Studies in Ephemera: Text and Image in Eighteenth-Century Print* (Lewisburg, PA: Bucknell University Press, 2013).

[5] See e.g. H. Love, *Scribal Publication in Seventeenth-Century England* (Oxford: Clarendon Press, 1993).

manuscript'.[6] Likewise, William A. Johnson comments on the 'creeping anachronism' of terms such as *book trade* or *bookseller* in studies of Greek and Latin papyri.[7] We must ask whether *publication* is, therefore, a fitting term. The first chapter of our book does that by examining three traditions with different degrees of connection to print – none at all, loose relations, and dependency. Jaakko Tahkokallio, noting the same 'ontological and epistemological insecurities' about referring to unprinted media as *publication*, suggests that rather than seek a strict definition, we can more happily observe different practices within a looser cluster of comparable phenomena. He suggests that:

> the most fruitful approach to the topic is not theoretical or categorical but configurational. In other words, we should study those concrete processes by which works were published in a manuscript context, with publishing by necessity remaining to some extent an open concept. We should probably simply be happy with the term "publishing" as a somewhat metaphorical concept; we have brought it in from a context in which it means the joint releasing and disseminating of content.[8]

We might evoke the way that the history of art encompasses phenomena not understood as 'art' at the time (religious artefacts, folk art) but that can be meaningfully compared for having shared properties or functions, whatever people at the time called them.

[6] S. Niskanen, 'Introduction', in S. Niskanen and V. Rovere, eds., *The Art of Publication from the Ninth to the Sixteenth Century* (Turnhout: Brepols, 2023), 12. For debate by medievalists, see e.g. D. Hobbins, *Authorship and Publicity before Print: Jean Gerson and the Transformation of Late Medieval Learning* (Philadelphia: University of Pennsylvania Press, 2009), 153–4; L. Tether, *Publishing the Grail in Medieval and Renaissance France* (Cambridge: Boydell and Brewer, 2017), 2–4.

[7] W. A. Johnson, *Bookrolls and Scribes in Oxyrhynchus* (Toronto: University of Toronto Press, 2004), 159.

[8] J. Tahkokallio, 'Theories, Categories, Configurations', in S. Niskanen and V. Rovere, eds., *The Art of Publication from the Ninth to the Sixteenth Century* (Turnhout: Brepols, 2023), 377.

This non-categorizing mode of understanding *publication* is the one we adopt in this book: we leave the concept flexible and instead explore multiple 'concrete processes'. Comparing different processes has led us not to any central theoretical definitions or categorizations; it has led us to appreciate the usefulness of the concept *publication* to draw together for comparison a variety of ways that people share texts with others. We emphasize the need to focus on that diversity and particularity, which are easier to see in any one instance when that instance is laid alongside others under one heading. With a loose definition, seemingly disparate examples disrupt the category of *publication*, as much as they decentre the importance of print. Tahkokallio suggested that, for instance, 'manuscript publishing is not as neat and self-evident a concept as print publishing is, or, at least, is commonly assumed to be'.[9] Nor, we would add, is any kind of publishing neatly defined and self-evident in the *what*, *how*, and *with what effect* that the three chapters of our book explore.

It is, nonetheless, interesting – perhaps reassuring – to remember that the word *publish* has a long history in English and in cognate forms in related languages and has equivalents that do similar work in other languages. For making texts public, Classical Latin employs, for instance, *edere* 'give out', *emittere* 'send out', and *divulgare* 'distribute among the people' (from *vulgus* 'crowd'). Similarly, in Classical Greek some of the relevant terms are *ekdídōmi* 'give out or away' (also used in the sense of giving away one's daughter in marriage), *diadídōmi* 'distribute', and *ekférō* 'bring out'. In Classical Latin, *publicare* is only attested in reference to books as late as the first century CE, and is more commonly used in the sense 'to make something public property'. The same applies to the Ancient Greek *dēmosióō* (from *dēmos*, 'the people'), with a similar meaning: its first clear use for literary works comes from the third century CE. In medieval Latin, *edere* is commonly employed as well as *publicare*.[10] What is interesting is the emphasis, etymologically, on movement, outwards or away from somebody

---

[9] Tahkokallio, 'Theories', 371.

[10] See quotations from medieval Latin by e.g. Tether, *Publishing the Grail*, 18; Niskanen, 'Introduction', 13; Hobbins, *Authorship*, 153; and P. Bourgain, 'La naissance officielle de l'œuvre: l'expression métaphorique de la mise au jour', in

(*ex*); in only some of the terms is there a connection to a wider 'public' as in *dēmosióō* or *divulgare*. As we note (in Chapter 3), a process might be compared to publishing without needing to address a wide 'public'. When the verb *publicare* moved through French into Middle English as *publish* in the 1400s, it could mean 'making public', for instance, in proclamations – and it certainly had nothing to do with, and preceded, the first printing press in Europe. However, from those earliest times *publish* had more varied meanings, and it was not an oxymoron in some uses in Middle English to refer to private publishing. An early attested instance urged people not to 'publish, en priue ne appert', any criticism of the authorities: the Middle English words mean that publishing should be neither 'in private nor public'.[11] Being public was not taken for granted. In Samuel Johnson's great dictionary of English in the 1700s, to *publish* could mean both 'to make generally and openly known' or 'to put forth a book into the world' – a physical process of disseminating.[12] There are similar varieties of uses in other, less closely related languages. For instance, in some early Tibetan written records, such as the inscriptions on the Zhol pillar from the mid eighth century CE, we find the term *kalung* (*bka' lung*) or *kashok* (*bka' shog*) for proclamations or official written documents in circulation, composed of the words 'speech'/'instruction' (*bka'*) and 'scripture'/'statement' (*lung*) or 'paper' (*shog*). Since the twelfth century at the latest, we also see a different and more figurative term *drildak* (*dril bsgrags*), composed of the noun 'scroll' ([*shog*] *dril*) and the transitive verb *drak* (*bsgrags*), 'to proclaim something', but also in the sense of 'to read out (publicly, before all assembled)'. In historical texts, *drildak* can therefore be translated as 'to proclaim [the contents of] a scroll'. From the middle of the twentieth century, *drildak* took on a further meaning and was used to translate Chinese *xuanchuan* or 'propaganda' into Tibetan but is also used to express

---

O. Weijers, ed., *Vocabulaire du livre et de l'écriture au Moyen Age* (Turnhout: Brepols, 1989), 195–205.

[11] R. W. Chambers and M. Daunt, eds., *A Book of London English, 1384–1425* (Oxford: Clarendon Press, 1931), 93 (line 5).

[12] S. Johnson, *A Dictionary of the English Language* (London: Knapton, 1755), s.v. 'To PUBLISH'.

'advertisement'. In addition, the Tibetan language has long used the verb and noun *par* to denote an actual impression, print, photograph, picture, and such like. Around the same time, modern terms such as *pardrem (par 'grems)* 'publishing, publication', composed of print (*par*) and the verb 'spread, display' (*'grems pa*) or the *trünkhang (skrun khang)* 'publishing house', have entered the modern Tibetan vocabulary. In Arabic, the verb 'to publish' (*nashara*) is based more generally on the act of spreading, unfolding, or extending an object, such as a piece of fabric or parchment. It could also refer to the spread of news and, similar to Tibetan, its proclamation before a group of people. Strikingly, the root of the verb *nashara* also has life-giving connotations: the act of plants producing leaves and, in a religious context, divine resurrection of the dead (*nushūr*).[13]

So many cultures do have equivalents of the word *publication* or *to publish*, but they have diverse connotations, often related to different media and material technologies of communication, and alluding to different degrees to a wider public, but sometimes without one or other of those implications. The shared set of equivalent terms makes it possible to compare different kinds of communication under the umbrella terms *publication* or *publishing* but also alerts us to the fact – central to our argument – that such a comparison only makes sense if we recognize the diversity of such publication, and do not try to find likenesses with late modern western uses of printing. The diverse periods and cultures that use terms equivalent to *publish* do so in a wider range of ways than any comparison to the contemporary print publishing industry might suggest. Inspired by such differences, in this book we do not simply rethink other media in comparison with modern print publishing. Instead, the variety of languages, cultures, periods and media brought together – in their jumbled diversity and vexing particularity – suggest that we expand the notion of publishing and cease to use late modern capitalist industrial book production to define it. That mode of publishing is only one among many possible.

To start unveiling the possibilities, in this first chapter, we begin by looking at some activities that are most readily comparable with the late

---

[13] E. W. Lane, *An Arabic-English Lexicon*, 8 vols. (London: Williams and Norgate, 1863–93), i, 2793–4.

modern printed publishing industry – cultures with known authors, an informed readership, libraries, professional makers of texts, and a reliance on writing and reading (albeit, in at least two of the case studies, in a complex relationship to orality). One tradition had all those ingredients of publishing but no printing; the other two interact with the printing industry to varying degrees. Throughout our book, each of these and the other cultural traditions that we consider is in other respects quite different from the world of printing and suggests that we decentre print from the study of publication. Some of them combine print with manuscript circulation: this happened for a long time after the introduction of printing not only in late fifteenth-century Germany (in our first chapter) but also, for instance, in the persistence of handwriting as a preliminary to printing, in authors' manuscripts, as in Samuel Beckett's archives (the final case study in our book). Other cultures used printing to support or document performance or rely on oral culture, as in the world of eighteenth-century London theatre or in Tibet in the same period (explored in Chapter 3).[14] Such cases show that there is not a firm divide between publication by printed and unprinted media, whether manuscript or performed. What about a culture that did not have any notion of printed publication to build on, such as the literary production on papyri in classical Greek and Roman antiquity: how does publication work entirely without printing?

---

[14] See also D. Wojahn, 'Inherited Stories, Timeless Wisdom: Intertextuality and Proverbs in the Aché Lhamo Namthar', *Journal of Tibetan Literature*, 3 (2024), 45–69.

Publication in Ancient Greece and Rome: No Print in Sight,
by Daria Kohler

How much does a book published in Rome in the year 2024 CE differ from another book, also published in Rome, but 2,000 years earlier? This question brings us, first and foremost, to the material aspect of book production. A modern book is usually characterized by the codex format – that is, it is made of sheets that had been folded a number of times, gathered and stitched or glued together, and covered by writing on both sides. In Rome in the year 24 CE, it would look quite different: the codex format had not yet fully claimed its place, and what was understood as a book was a roll: a long sheet produced by gluing single sheets of papyrus to each other until the necessary length was reached, with the writing placed in columns running down the shorter side, its back blank (Figure 1).[15]

The process itself brings out an even more important difference: in the pre-print era, trained scribes copied a text by hand, which meant that each copy was an individual artefact; no two books were completely identical. There was still an expectation of a certain format: for example, prose texts would be 'justified' in their columns, to use a modern term, while poetry was 'flush-left'.[16] Usually, literary texts would be copied in a type of handwriting scholars now call 'a book hand', while letters and documents were penned in a variety of cursive; yet this is not a hard divide, but rather a strong tendency.[17] The level of professionalism of the copyists differed as well. Moreover, nothing stopped one from copying a literary text themselves if they wished (even if we do not have many such cases) and while ancient literature knows some famous editors – that is, scholars who worked with what were already older texts – as well as a few famous booksellers, there was no equivalent of modern publishing houses.[18]

---

[15] The latest monograph on the ancient book, its history and material realisation is L. Del Corso, *Il libro nel mondo antico. Archeologia e storia (secoli VII a.C.- IV d.C.)* (Roma: Carocci, 2022).

[16] Johnson, *Bookrolls*, 101.

[17] The famous papyrus of *Constitution of the Athenians* (London: British Library, inv.131v) is copied by four scribes, and none of them uses a book hand: Johnson, *Bookrolls*, 157.

[18] E.g. A. Dortmund, *Römisches Buchwesen um die Zeitenwende: War T. Pomponius Atticus (110–32 v. Chr.) Verleger?* (Wiesbaden: Harrassowitz, 2001).

Figure 1 A papyrus with Plato's *Phaedrus* from Oxyrhynchus (modern El-Bahnasa, Egypt), dated to the late second century CE (P.Oxy XVII 2102; fragment). The preserved part of the roll carries nine columns of text. © Egypt Exploration Society. Courtesy of The Egypt Exploration Society and the Faculty of Classics, University of Oxford.

Before moving on to the publication of books, we need to situate the papyrus roll in the literary context of its time: as in other cultures and other periods, texts could very well be created and made public without the use of writing. Many of the genres of what we now call ancient Greek and Latin literature were chiefly oral: epic poetry, speeches, hymns and odes, and tragedies and comedies did not first reach their audiences on a papyrus roll but were listened to in courts, at festivals, or in the theatre. Yet we also see books, both in the written record and in the archaeological finds. One of the earliest Greek literary papyri is of the lyric poet Timotheos, whose main activity would be performing at poetic competitions; it has multiple features of a book roll, starting with the script, paratextual signs such as the *coronis* (a mark indicating the end of the narrative part), and a side note that could have been added by a reader or copyist.[19] Another among the oldest surviving Greek book fragments, the famous Derveni papyrus, preserved due to the carbonization process brought about by a funeral pyre, carries a commentary on an Orphic poem, more likely to be needed for study and not for performance.[20] The two modes of publication, written and oral, are not mutually exclusive.

Books could be given as a gift; copied on request; bought at a bookseller's shop in a city, or from a travelling bookseller coming to a market; they could also be read in private and public libraries. In all of these situations, the book in question can probably be considered published. However, the oral dimension does not stop complicating the picture. In addition to a variety of ways to make sure their books reached the relevant audiences, authors often gave readings, which could constitute the first public appearance of the text or contribute to improving a work still in progress; readings of the former type filled an important niche in the cultural life of the Roman literary-minded public.[21] It is certain that, at least for some authors and some texts, such 'performances' played an important role in making their work public. In this context, it may seem that the very term *publication* is either inapplicable or should be extended to include oral performances as well.

If we look at the extant papyri, the closest one can get to the real books, we can see a whole world of literary activity going on. There are copies with large margins and wide spaces between columns and those with lines crammed on top of each other; there are annotations and marginalia;

---

[19] Berlin, Preußischer Kulturbesitz, P.Berol. inv. 9875 (https://berlpap.smb.museum/ 02776/). The papyrus was first edited by U. von Wilamowitz-Moellendorff, *Timotheos, Die Perser* (Leipzig: Hinrichs, 1903). See also J. H. Hordern, *The Fragments of Timotheus of Miletus* (Oxford: Oxford University Press, 2002).

[20] Recent edition: M. E. Kotwick, *Der Papyrus von Derveni* (Berlin: De Gryuter, 2017).

[21] G. Binder, 'Öffentliche Autorenlesungen: Zur Kommunikation zwischen Römischen Autoren und ihrem Publikum', in G. Binder and K. Ehlich, eds., *Kommunikation durch Zeichen und Wort* (Trier: Wissenschaftlicher Verlag, 1995), 265–332. For various ways of publication, see also T. Kleberg, 'Commercio librario ed editoria nel mondo antico', in G. Cavallo, *Libri, editori e pubblico nel mondo antico* (Roma: Laterza, 1975), 43–5.

there are papyri that bear traces of composition, potential and confirmed authorial drafts, and many more papyri with signs of corrections made to a known text; finally, there is evidence of the practice of anthologizing: creating new textual collections on the basis of existing texts.

What exactly is, then, ancient book publication? Was it a recognizable concept for authors and readers of papyrus rolls? While both Greek and Latin employ an array of verbs and expressions that mean something along the lines of 'making public' (*edere* 'give out'; *in medium dare* 'put into the open'; *dēmosióō* 'give to public use'; *eis tò fōs ekférō* 'bring to light'), none of them are restricted in their meaning to the more technical 'putting a book into wider circulation'; this is also the case for other languages (as has just been shown). *Edere* and its synonyms can designate any action resulting in the text becoming available to a wide(r) audience, not only one initiated by its author. In the absence of the printing press, the lack of specific vocabulary, and the importance of oral transmission, it is alluring to claim that there was no such thing as ancient publishing, and that papyrus rolls, produced in smaller quantities and sometimes used to facilitate an oral performance of a text, played a comparatively insignificant role in the literary landscape of their time. This claim does not hold ground on both counts; publication, meaning the process in which a text reaches its audience, was a matter of considerable importance, and the bookroll did play a significant role in it.

Greek and Roman authors were well aware of the difference between published and unpublished. In Plato's dialogue *Parmenides*, the philosopher Zeno replies to Socrates' criticism of his work as follows:

> It is because of such a great zeal for rivalry that I wrote it when I was young, and someone stole the writing, so that I did not even have the chance to decide whether it should be brought to light or not. Thus, Socrates, it escapes you that it was written by a young man out of competitiveness, not by an old man out of ambition.[22]

---

[22] Translation my own. See Plato, *Cratylus. Parmenides. Greater Hippias. Lesser Hippias*, ed. H. N. Fowler (Cambridge, MA: Harvard University Press, 1926), *Parmenides*, 128d–e.

In the broader setting of the dialogue Zeno and Parmenides, his teacher, come to Athens and bring along Zeno's works, which attracts to their place of stay the interested philosophers, including Socrates. Zeno is reading aloud, and Socrates asks him to repeat a passage before commenting. It is during this reading – an oral performance – that Socrates and the others hear the work for the first time. However, the explanation about the context of its composition introduces an alternative way of distribution, unauthorized and irreversible. In Zeno's defence, he claims that he was deprived of the possibility of deciding to make his written work public – to *publish* it?

When a book starts to circulate, there is no way of stopping it. Comments and complaints about the work 'escaping' the author without their permission or even against their will are common in Greek and Latin literature. While in our example, one can question the importance of the written copy, in many of Cicero's letters, there is no doubt that he is concerned with working on a *book*. A famous passage from his correspondence is an outburst against his friend Atticus, who, it seems, allowed a common acquaintance to make a copy of a book that would be dedicated to someone else. Cicero states clearly that this is out of order: 'Do you find it right to give it to someone else before Brutus, to whom I'm dedicating it on your advice?'[23] The dedicatee is the person who should receive the new book first, something that Atticus endangered: if the lending and copying continued, the book would have been 'out' too early.

Along with the impossibility of restricting the reach of a book's readership comes the near impossibility of changing its text. In Latin literature, and especially in Latin poetry, the author's decision to publish and its irreversibility became commonplace. Horace's famous line *nescit vox missa reverti* – 'the word sent out cannot return' – is now often used as a proverb referring to taking back what one has said, but in its original context it is a comment on the inability of a writer to conceal anything they have created.[24] If a text is already out there, all that remains for the author is 'damage control': issuing comments and corrections where possible. So the

---

[23] Cicero, *Letters to Atticus*, ed. D. R. Shackleton Bailey, 4 vols. (Cambridge, MA: Harvard University Press, 1999), letter 327 (XIII.21a).

[24] Horace, *Satires, Epistles, The Art of Poetry*, ed. H. Rushton Fairclough (Cambridge, MA: Harvard University Press, 1926), *Art of Poetry*, line 390.

Greek historian Diodorus (of the first century BCE) says in the preface to his *Historical Library* that some books were stolen while he worked on the whole and started circulating before they were corrected, and that he should not be held responsible for the errors found therein.[25]

While introducing changes was largely out of the question – though authors could try to do so – copying by hand also meant that nothing was error-proof.[26] The further away from the 'original', the more changes could have occurred. Looking for a copy with a good, reliable text was important for educated readers, and Cicero complained in a letter to his brother about the low quality of the Greek books available on offer.[27] This feature lent the first copy a special value: unlike, perhaps, the collectors' interest in the first editions, the first copy of a Greek or Latin literary work was simply better, by definition. The existence of such copies was claimed by ancient scholars who refer to them when looking for the support of authority.[28] And we may even encounter cases of author–reader engagement that illustrate the same. One such example is Pliny's letter in which he responds to a request from a reader to 'inspect and correct' (*recognoscere* and *emendare*) his own books.[29] In asking the still-living author to 'proofread' their copy, readers attempt to bring it closer to the ideal.

The moment of publication in antiquity thus joins something irreversible – the availability of a text to a public beyond the author's influence – with something fleeting: namely, the unstable text that will keep changing on a smaller or larger scale as it is passed down from copy to copy.

---

[25] Diodorus Siculus, *Library of History*, ed. F. R. Walton et al., 12 vols. (Cambridge, MA: Harvard University Press, 1963–71), Book 40, fr. 8.

[26] On authorial variants, see e.g. G. Pasquali, *Storia della tradizione e critica del testo* (Florence: Le Monnier, 1934), 396–465.

[27] Cicero, *Letters to Quintus and Brutus*, ed. D. R. Shackleton Bailey (Cambridge, MA: Harvard University Press, 2002), letter 24 (III.4).

[28] In Aulus Gellius, *Attic Nights*, ed. J. C. Rolfe, 3 vols. (Cambridge, MA: Harvard University Press, 1946–52), Book 13, 21.4, a grammarian supports his claim regarding Vergil's use of the forms *urbis* or *urbes* by saying that he saw a book 'corrected in his own hand'.

[29] Pliny the Younger, *Letters*, ed. B. Radice, 2 vols. (Cambridge, MA: Harvard University Press, 1969), Book 4, letter 26.

Manuscripts in Germany in Response to Print,
by Natascha Domeisen

While handwritten text production has seen its fair share of changes in format and material in various writing cultures, the advent of moveable type has been historically viewed as a watershed, a dramatic turning point in the history of writing and consequently, publication. It is easy to imagine manuscripts disappearing, unable to withstand the competition. The development of printing in the West, however, also gave rise to a diverse range of transitional book-objects that hovered between the manuscript and the printed book. Manuscripts, as well as other forms of textual production, such as inscription and performance (as the next case study will show), were not obliterated, taking on new functions instead.

Technical developments in printing throughout the late Middle Ages produced a diverse multimedia landscape, particularly across manuscripts and printed books. Although manuscripts and printed books in western Europe shared the codex form, they were, by nature of their manual application of script or technical application of print, different media. From their production process, both manuscripts and printed books possess inherent and medium-specific regularities and conventions that formed and became established through a continuous exchange between book users and makers.

Early printed books first mirrored and followed conventions established by manuscripts, beginning with the use of parchment or vellum before the switch to paper. Adhering to a well-trodden path was not a simple imitation game but rather made books created with a new technology accessible to readers familiar with an older medium. This is evident in early printed editions of German vernacular texts, such as the heroic tale of the giant *Sigenot* or the fairytale-like story of *Melusine*, which in their content, script, layout, and image placement followed manuscript conventions.[30] The books printed in Europe before 1501 (known as incunabula) and even in subsequent decades referred back to manuscripts in their aesthetics. The

---

[30] H. Lähnemann and T. Kröner, 'Die Überlieferung des Sigenot: Bildkonzeptionen im Vergleich von Handschrift, Wandmalerei und Frühdrucken', *Jahrbuch der Oswald von Wolkenstein-Gesellschaft*, 14 (2004), 175–88.

individual elements of a book, through their complex interplay, worked together to form a complete and 'readable' book-object.

With the shift from courtly to urban book production in the late Middle Ages, and the flourishing of printing presses in cities such as Mainz, Strasbourg, and Frankfurt, the printed book started to carve out its own niche in the quickly changing media landscape of fifteenth- and sixteenth-century Europe. The development of the printed book slowly started to diverge from manuscript-making and established its own conventions born of its specific technicalities of production. These print-specific developments included features such as title pages, page numbering, and new types of quire signatures to facilitate coopera-tion within the workshop. In a continuous exchange, the makers of printed books and their audience started to establish new rules for their use. Publishers and printers tried to capture movements in the market, adjusting their new products to the needs and interests of a growing audience.

The diverging developments of the two media meant that the printed book and manuscript started to fulfil differing purposes and offered new ways of usage. The German Emperor Elect Maximilian I (1459–1519) always carried a copy of *Sigenot* on his person during his travels, a cheapish printed octavo edition.[31] (This format was a full-sized sheet of paper folded three times, giving sixteen leaves roughly 15 to 21 cm high and 10 to 12 cm wide.) He was immortalized as having accumulated one of the most renowned and costly manuscript collections in the world, which included various luxury copies of vernacular works, including another copy of *Sigenot*. Cheaply produced prints with high print-runs and numerous editions, such as pamph-lets or single-leaf prints, were literally read to bits as a means of edification and entertainment. On the other hand, expensive illuminated manuscripts fulfilled additional functions, among others guiding the daily religious prac-tices of affluent lay persons and religious communities.

While decorated manuscripts were out of reach for most of the popula-tion, printed books became an attainable product to an extent, while still being able to cater to the top end of the market through their text selection, high-quality woodcuts, and other decorative elements. Despite the empha-sis by later commentators on the divergence of the two media, they were

---

[31] Lähnemann and Kröner, 'Überlieferung', 183.

never opposed but rather complemented each other. This is demonstrated by the fact that skills needed to produce one or the other were often transferable, and in the early era of printing, scribes, miniaturists, and artists often worked on both products, switching between the scriptorium and the print workshop.[32] This is just another example of exchange in the late Middle Ages, a flourishing multi-media age in which materials were transposed from literary texts into tapestry, ivory carvings, woodwork, coins, and stained glass. Artists were used to adapting materials to the limitations of a particular medium and for the use of a specific audience.

While the move from manuscript to printed book seems intuitive, it was not irreversible. On the contrary, printed books and materials were sometimes transcribed back into manuscript. The various reasons are often difficult to establish exactly, but personal preference for one medium above the other seems to have been a determining factor. This preference can be observed in late medieval aristocratic commissions of manuscripts instead of printed books. The term *copying* does not capture how much was changed when a printer transferred a manuscript copy-text into type. In the moment of copying, the scribe or printer-publisher undertook a media transfer whose multi-layered processes can no longer be grasped, and which transformed both the details of the text being transcribed and its value and significance.

A great example of the media transfer between printed book and manuscript can be found in the collection of Princess Margaret of Savoy (1420–79).[33] She was a keen bibliophile who had grown up surrounded by renowned patrons, among them the famous duke of Berry. During Margaret's third and final marriage, to Duke Ulrich V of Württemberg, she commissioned a series of vernacular German manuscripts between 1470 and her death in 1479. Eleven manuscripts are still extant (at Heidelberg University Library) and tell the

[32] H. Lähnemann, 'From Print to Manuscript: The Case of a Workshop in Stuttgart around 1475', in M. C. Fischer and W. A. Kelly, eds., *The Book in Germany* (Edinburgh: Merchiston, 2010), 17–34; N. H. Ott, 'Die Handschriften-Tradition im 15. Jahrhundert', in B. Tiemann, ed., *Die Buchkultur im 15. und 16. Jahrhundert* (Hamburg: Maximilian-Gesellschaft, 1995), 47–124.

[33] P. Rückert, K. Oschema, and A. Thaller, *Die Tochter des Papstes: Margarethe von Savoyen* (Stuttgart: Kohlhammer, 2020).

fascinating story of their patroness and her literary interests.[34] Most of the texts in her collection either were already available in print, such as *Sigenot* (mentioned earlier) or *Pontus und Sidonie*, a courtly romance, or went on to become bestsellers in printed form such as *Herpin*, a medieval prose epos. All three were vernacular stories available in a variety of European languages and in wide circulation in Germany and France. Despite their evident availability in print and their affordability, Margaret commissioned the so-called Henfflin workshop, named after the only identifiable scribe, with the creation of manuscript copies.[35] The workshop, most likely an ad hoc consortium made up of German craftsmen and artists, had been assembled especially for the commission by the princess.[36]

As the basis for the manuscripts of vernacular German, the Henfflin workshop used printed editions whose influences are tangible not only in the texts but also in their layout. However, there are changes too: while later German printed editions of *Sigenot*, *Herpin*, and *Pontus und Sidonia* included only a limited number of woodcuts, the manuscripts were often decorated with one illustration per page, conveying her particular understanding of what could be the distinctive offering of courtly manuscripts even in a time of print. The need for an illustration on every page creates a unique object, drawing on print but employing manuscript to cater to a courtly audience. While luxury printed books, such as *Theuerdank*, commissioned by the aforementioned Maximilian I, did exist, they were eclipsed by the sheer number of elaborate manuscript Books of Hours produced for patrons in Flanders, France, Italy, and elsewhere until the late sixteenth century. The manuscript was still the medium of choice, at least for the nobility, when it came to their daily liturgical offices, private devotion and entertainment.

---

[34] H. Lähnemann, 'Margarethe von Savoyen in ihren literarischen Beziehungen', in *Encomia-Deutsch*, 2 (2002), 159–73.

[35] Named from a colophon in Heidelberg, University Library, MS cpg 67, f. 102r. See U. Spyra and M. Effinger, 'Schwäbische Werkstatt Des Ludwig Henfflin', Universitätsbibliothek Heidelberg: Bibliotheca Palatina online, https://digi .ub.uni-heidelberg.de/de/bpd/glanzlichter/oberdeutsche/henfflin.html.

[36] P. Rudolph, 'Buchkunst im Zeitalter des Medienwandels. Die deutschsprachigen Bibelcodices der Henfflin-Werkstatt vor dem Hintergrund der spätmittelalterlichen Ikonographie' (MA thesis, KU Eichstätt-Ingolstadt, 2008), 25–6.

Printed books were transferred into manuscript form even in the case of substantial literary works, such as the fantastic and satirical *Mörin*, which consists of more than 6,000 lines of verse. The work was initially written in 1453 by the German knight and poet Hermann of Sachsenheim and dedicated to the Duchess Mechthild von der Pfalz. Manuscript copies of *Mörin* remain simple and mostly unadorned. In turn, multiple printed editions of the text were created between 1512 and 1565; but in 1538 the text of the first printed edition of 1512 was copied by hand into a manuscript. The lavish decoration of the printed edition was not included, and the text stripped down to its textual bones, as it was originally composed by the author in 1453. This renewed media transfer clearly contrasted with the luxurious nature of the printed editions of *Mörin*, which included twenty-two opulent and high-quality woodcuts. The divergence between the manuscript and printed tradition of *Mörin* hints at different audiences and specific uses of each medium.

The examples of the Henfflin manuscripts and *Mörin* show that while printed products were readily available, manuscript and print existed side by side in a fruitful and beneficial relationship. Both media profited from each other and adapted and absorbed developments from the other medium to suit the varying habits of particular late medieval audiences. Print similarly interacted in this way with non-textual media such as dramatic performance (as in the case studies of eighteenth-century theatre below). Despite the rise of printed books, manuscripts would not lose their status as the default medium for the first few decades after the introduction of printing with movable type. Their continued hegemony and heritage is underlined by the fact that incunabula and early printed books still followed their conventions, despite heralding a fundamental change in the media landscape.

The use of manuscript might seem like a turn away from publication to a more private use of the text; but it continues to expand the text's dissemination, rather than to contract it, albeit at a slower pace than printing could. Manuscript was the initial medium of the poet of *Mörin*, Hermann of Sachsenheim. And even when printed editions were copied 'back' into manuscripts, those manuscripts transmitted the text to a different audience with different financial means, taste or intellectual requirements. Like the papyri of Greek and Latin literature, such manuscripts are clearly doing similar work, each for different, specific circumstances – both before and after printing was introduced.

Performance as Publication in the Eighteenth Century, by Katie Noble

It is, then, easy to identify instances of textual dissemination that are clearly comparable with – albeit always subtly different in intention and effect from – printed publication; the makers of papyri and manuscripts, even the ones copied from printed books, circulate texts in physical form, but to different audiences. Such has been a standard part of the expanded sense of 'publication' in recent scholarship. Can we move beyond physical media and consider theatrical and other forms of performance as modes of publication? Such an expansion would make sense in the twenty-first century when various media, notably video embedded in social media and other platforms, allow people to circulate recordings of their words that might once have been shared in writing. Forms of performance, such as song and spoken announcements (in later sections of this book), might similarly challenge publication as exclusively relating to written dissemination.

In the eighteenth century, publication was not limited to printing or manuscript. According to Samuel Johnson's 1755 *Dictionary of the English Language*, to publish is simply to make something 'generally and openly known'. For example, preaching, a primarily oral tradition is defined by Johnson as 'to proclaim or publish'.[37] Dramatic performance was similarly linked to concepts of publication.[38] One such case can be seen in the backlash against the Licensing Act of 1737 in Britain. The 1737 Licensing Act introduced a process of censorship to the publication of new stage dramas. Resulting from heightened political unrest at the turn of the century, this piece of legislation, enacted under King George II and Britain's first prime minister Robert Walpole, required all new plays to be submitted to the Lord Chamberlain's office for approval. Politician and author of letters Phillip Dormer Stanhope, the fourth earl of Chesterfield, made a speech to Parliament against the introduction of the act. In his speech, Lord Chesterfield argued that the proposed Licensing Act was

---

[37] Johnson, *Dictionary*, s.v. 'To PUBLISH' and 'To PREACH'.

[38] J. Wessel, *Owning Performance | Performing Ownership: Literary Property and the Eighteenth-Century British Stage* (Ann Arbor: University of Michigan Press, 2022), 38.

unnecessary as the government already had recourse to deal with libellous or overly critical plays through legislation aimed at print, stating there is 'no Difficulty to prove who is the *Publisher* of it, the *Player* himself is the *Publisher*'.[39] Chesterfield identified the stage performer as an active participant in publication; in speaking the words on the stage, it is the performer who makes them public.

In her investigation of performance and literary ownership, Jane Wessel endorses a definition of publication that avoids an exclusive association with print. She instead invokes publication 'in its broadest sense of making ideas public', in which 'performance function[s] as a way of producing knowledge'.[40] In this book, we take a similar view of publication in which it is deliberately unmoored from the printed page. As examples from eighteenth-century theatre show, performance can be considered a type of publication, subjected to the same kinds of censorship that have attempted to stifle its ability to disseminate knowledge and ideas to the public, especially those critical of the state.

Throughout the early eighteenth century in Britain, the state and Crown had growing concerns about potentially dangerous political liberty during a time of significant unrest. The threat of further Jacobite rebellion was looming, and Walpole feared the theatre as a potential avenue through which perilous criticism and even violent opposition could spread.[41] Indeed, political satire was a common sight on the eighteenth-century London stage. And even before the passing of the Licensing Act in 1737, the government had reacted to this potential risk with censorship. This was the case with John Gay's play *Polly*, the intended sequel to his highly successful *The Beggar's Opera* (1728). *The Beggar's Opera* is considered to be one the century's most successful plays, offering comment on both the contemporary vogue for Italian opera and Walpole's corrupt government.

---

[39] Quoted in *A New Miscellany for the Year 1737* (London: Osborn, 1737), 18, original emphasis.

[40] Wessel, *Owning Performance*, 5.

[41] D. Thomas, 'The 1737 Licensing Act and its Impact', in J. Swindells and D. F. Taylor, eds., *The Oxford Handbook of the Georgian Theatre 1737–1832* (Oxford: Oxford University Press, 2014), 93–5.

In December 1728, *Polly* was banned from rehearsal. In his preface for the 1729 printed edition, Gay explains how:

> After Mr. *Rich* and I were agreed upon terms and conditions
> for bringing this Piece on the Stage, and that every Thing
> was ready for a Rehearsal; The Lord Chamberlain sent an
> order from the Country to prohibit Mr. *Rich* to suffer any
> Play to be rehears'd upon his Stage till it had been first of all
> supervis'd by his Grace.[42]

Gay had previously been identified as being associated with the political opposition and so it was in the state's interest to confirm whether his new play contained any inflammatory content before allowing it to be performed. Gay later heard that his play would not be allowed, the decision being delivered 'without any reasons assign'd'.[43] However, the censorship faced by *Polly* became the subject of public intrigue, and, sensing an opportunity, Gay contracted his printer to produce 10,500 copies of the play. Luckily for Gay, the Licensing Act only applied to the *performance* of plays, not their printing. And so, despite *Polly*'s controversy, the 1729 edition of the printed play was incredibly popular, and Gay made significant profit from it.[44] The differing treatment of the play's two forms suggests that performance was considered as a potentially damning form of publication, just as dangerous as the pen or printing press.[45]

The censorship heralded by Gay's *Polly* was later codified by the 1737 Licensing Act. Not only did the act require all new plays to be submitted to the Lord Chamberlain's office at least fourteen days prior to their first performance, but also all new playhouses were required to seek approval

---

[42] J. Gay, *Polly; an Opera: Being the Second Part of The Beggar's Opera* (London: no. pub., 1729), i, original emphasis.

[43] Gay, *Polly*, iv.

[44] C. Winton, *John Gay and the London Theatre* (Lexington: University Press of Kentucky, 1993), 131–5.

[45] The play was eventually performed at the Haymarket in June 1777, long after Gay's death.

from the office, greatly hindering the opening of new theatrical venues. Any unlicensed playhouse found to be staging performances would find its manager charged a then-hefty fine of £50 per offence. The effects of the Licensing Act were swift and far-reaching. Theatre historian David Thomas notes, 'Almost overnight, the managers of London's unlicensed playhouses were deprived of their livelihood.' Precedence was given to London's two patent theatres, Covent Garden and Drury Lane, effectively establishing a monopoly that was fiercely defended by the two theatres' managers over the ensuing years.[46] Understandably, it also had a significant effect on the writing of new dramas and entertainments. It has been estimated that, during the management of David Garrick at Drury Lane, only around two new mainpiece plays were staged each season.[47] It was safer to restage old favourites or otherwise mount revivals of Shakespeare which could abate the risk of censorship. Despite the fact that many older plays, including Shakespeare, contained potentially challenging ideas, it seems that the main concern was for contemporary new writing that might address the current political moment and encourage criticism.

If we understand publication, then, as making something public to some audience or other, then indeed the theatre had potential for the widespread publication of such ideas. After the Restoration of the Stuart monarchy in 1660, which had followed a period of Puritan republican government, there had been a reactionary antitheatrical movement against the stage as encouraging blasphemous and otherwise distasteful behaviour The passing of the Licensing Act, at least in part, responded to such commentary and by the end of the eighteenth century, similar arguments were being made about the reading of novels. It seems that on a grander scale, the risk of the theatre was less in the size of its audience, than in its ability to verbalise – figuratively and, more importantly, literally – ideas seen to challenge the status quo.

Apart from some early resistance, this new 'culture of censorship' was quickly internalized by playwrights and, as a result, very few plays were

---

[46] Thomas, '1737 Licensing Act', 96–97.

[47] R. W. Schoch, '"A Supplement to Public Laws": Arthur Murphy, David Garrick, and 'Hamlet, with Alterations", *Theatre Journal*, 57 (2005), 21–32 (24).

actually refused licences or banned completely following the passing of the Act.[48] Instead, censored plays were given revisions – sometimes minor, sometimes extensive – and received licences in a 'cleaner and much less political' state.[49] In the few cases where a play was banned under the Act, such as with Henry Brooke's *Gustavus Vasa* (1739), a playwright may have used a play's print publication as a way to recoup any financial losses from the cancelled performance. This was one risk of the fact that the Licensing Act only applied to the performance of plays. In his speech against the act, Lord Chesterfield had warned that:

> When my L[ord] C[hamberlain] has *marked* a Play with his *Refusal*, may it not be *printed*? *Will* it not be *printed* with *double* the Advantage, when it shall be insinuated, that it was *refused* for having some Character or Strokes of Wit or Satire in it, that were *not suffered* to come on the *Stage*? And will not the Printer set the *Refusal* in his Title-Page as a *Mark of Value*?[50]

This is exactly what happened in the case of Brooke's play. *Gustavus Vasa*, a historical play concerning the liberation of Sweden from the Kingdom of Denmark, was banned following Walpole's anxieties about being compared to its antagonist. It has been contended that the play was 'notable for [its] critical treatment of imperial invasion and domination'.[51] The title page of Brooke's play, rejected by the Lord Chamberlain in 1738 and printed in 1739, tempts its reader with the promise of exclusive access to its censored content: the play presented 'as it was to have been acted' at Drury Lane, in

---

[48] D. O'Shaughnessy, 'Introduction: Theatre Censorship and Georgian Cultural History', in D. O'Shaughnessy, ed., *The Censorship of Eighteenth-Century Theatre: Playhouses and Prohibition, 1737–1843* (Cambridge: Cambridge University Press, 2023), 1–32 (7).

[49] M. J. Kinservik, *Disciplining Satire: The Censorship of Satiric Comedy on the Eighteenth-Century London Stage* (Lewisburg: Bucknell University Press, 2002), 30.

[50] *A New Miscellany*, 20, original emphasis.

[51] B. Orr, 'Theatrical Censorship and Empire', in O'Shaughnessy, ed., *Censorship*, 102.

Chesterfield's words, 'as a *Mark of Value*'.[52] With Brooke's *Gustavus Vasa* and Gay's *Polly*, print is the playwright's only chance at publication and, crucially, an opportunity to take back control over their contentious literary property.[53]

Similarly, playwrights of an edited play could use print publication as a method of circulating its earlier, unedited form, in effect, offering the printed play as a 'second edition' of a drama's initial publication in performance. However, this was not particularly common. It has been observed that there was rather 'a remarkable reticence on the part of the playwrights' and that, in most cases, printed plays followed the same version as was performed on the stage, including any changes made by the Lord Chamberlain's office.[54]

It has previously been claimed that at least 88 per cent of plays submitted to the Lord Chamberlain's office under the Licensing Act were also printed.[55] However, despite their existence in print, it is impossible to access what was actually performed on the stage. Performance, by its very nature, is ephemeral and so, to understand and interpret historical performance, theatre historians must turn to forms of print evidence such as playbills, advertisements, prints and the playtexts themselves. Perhaps we often think of publication as printing precisely because these printed sources are the forms that most easily survive the passing of time. However, as we will continue to argue, performance itself can be considered a kind of publication through which the performer, with their voice rather than a pen, expresses to the audience their knowledge or ideas.

---

[52] H. Brooke, *Gustavus Vasa, the Deliverer of His Country: A Tragedy – As It Was to Have Been Acted at the Theatre-Royal in Drury-Lane* (London: Dodsley, 1739).

[53] On the other end of the spectrum, some playwrights withheld the printing of their plays to protect their literary property from wily copiers. See Wessel, *Owning Performance*, 39–40.

[54] M. J. Kinservik, 'The Dialectics of Print and Performance after 1737', in J. Swindells and D. Taylor, eds., *Oxford Handbook of the Georgian Theatre*, 123–39 (139).

[55] R. W. Bevis, *The Laughing Tradition: Stage Comedy in Garrick's Day* (Athens, GA: University of Georgia Press, 1980), 26.

2 Personal Agency and Its Limits

In the world of the eighteenth-century theatre, the tension between written record and performance also raises questions about the agency in textual dissemination. There were roles not only for authors but also for actors, not to mention censorial Lord Chancellors, in the dissemination of play texts; and there were roles for printers and other entrepreneurs in publishing the performances. Each method of disseminating one's creative work to the public rested on the originator of the words or deeds, the author or actor, as well as on multiple agents, even ones which might seem 'passive' such as dedicatees – what Jaakko Tahkokallio calls a 'publishing circle'.[56] Those multiple agents of fame in the eighteenth-century theatre thus exemplify a key puzzle for understanding publication: who facilitates it and controls it, given the technological constraints of different media, and the diverse societies and cultures in which those media are used?

Even in print, the process of publication involves a wide variety of agents. That puts into question the common presumption about print, that it fosters freedom of speech. Jeff Jarvis notes that the technology and economics of printing gave the users of the press 'the power to decide who had a voice in media's finite space and time.' He, like many heralds of digital media, contrasts 'the internet, which tore open media's container' and allowed mass participation in publishing.[57] It is true that some digital technologies, notably self-publishing and social media, do allow many more people to disseminate their words, pictures and videos, and allow some to share them very widely.

It would be tempting to glance back across Jarvis's 'Gutenberg Parenthesis' (with which we began) and find a similar freedom of expression before, and alongside, the often regulated medium of printing. Digital media seem worth comparing with handwriting, carving and speech because, for all their differences, some of them share a particular 'affordance' or capability: they are means of communication that people seem to operate for themselves, without necessarily requiring prohibitively expensive or easily overmastered equipment, like the printing press. Folk-singers or letter-writers make texts for themselves like

---

[56] J. Tahkokallio, *The Anglo-Norman Historical Canon Publishing and Manuscript Culture* (Cambridge: Cambridge University Press, 2019), 8–9.

[57] Jarvis, *Gutenberg Parenthesis*, 149. On the idea of print fostering freedom of speech, see Jarvis, *Gutenberg Parenthesis*, 14.

the users of 'desktop publishing' or creators of video blogs. But, once again, the particularity of any one example soon reveals that people's agency in publishing beyond the press is not merely a question of empowerment: their agency is sometimes shared, sometimes negotiated, sometimes compromised, sometimes limited. First, in some cases people's words are not entirely their own: they can compile, adapt or perform words that are partially those of other people, or of traditional or commonplace forms. Second, in many cases people's words are mediated by professionals, such as carvers, scribes or information technologists or by advanced skills, for instance in musical performance (as in our case studies in this chapter), and shaped by cultural conventions and controls – political, technological, financial and otherwise, both known and unrecognized. (Another interesting story would be the circulation of 'samizdat' or underground publication of banned works in communist East Germany, where dissident artists seemed to be publishing their work beyond the press, but later found that their activities were being tolerated and even facilitated by state authorities.)[58] In unprinted media as in print, authors rarely self-publish, in the sense of doing so entirely by themselves.

The roles of multiple agents involved in the circulating of texts is particularly well explored for the making of manuscripts before and overlapping with printing. Publishing in the manuscripts of the medieval west 'was a social act, which involved third parties in addition to those two core agents, an author and his or her intended audience'; the patron was often the person empowered to circulate the work.[59] A key recognition in recent scholarship about manuscripts has been that medieval scribes readily altered the texts they copied, in ways formerly disparaged but now acclaimed as creative 'variance' and even authorship.[60] This admixture of different people's agency, espied in many manuscript texts of the European Middle Ages, is made even more complex when we consider that these manuscript works were also shared orally in various kinds of performance. As in the eighteenth-century theatre, such mediations raise questions not only about what counts as publication but also whose words are being published.

---

[58] A. Ní Chroidheáin, ed., *Dangerous Creations* (Oxford: Taylor Institution, 2022).

[59] Quoting Niskanen, 'Introduction', 15. See also Tether, *Publishing the Grail*, 20.

[60] M. Fisher, *Scribal Authorship and the Writing of History in Medieval England* (Columbus: Ohio State University Press, 2012).

Carols, Authorship, and Agency, by Micah Mackay

Many medieval works present a multitude of agencies, as they move between different textual and performed modes of dissemination. One example is the Middle English carol, a form of song whose remnants survive largely within fifteenth-century manuscripts of song and verse. The carols reveal how many different agents might be involved in 'publication' both in the book and in performance.[61]

Middle English carols not only concern Christmas; they are wide-ranging, from reflective liturgical pieces to bawdy drinking songs, and would suit varied environments. Many carols begin with commands such as *sing we* or *make we joy*, words that seem to be spoken by, or to, a group that has assembled for religious celebration or merry-making.[62] A carol comprises a set of verses and a shorter burden, which is sung at the start and repeated after every verse. It is generally accepted that the verses were for soloists while the burden was for a group.[63] The carol's structure, therefore, specifically encourages those assembled to participate. This repetition of the burden is also a memory device, transmitting the message and melody to the minds of those listening to and repeating its words. This structure could thus be seen as enabling fresh 'publication' of a revised or varied carol – and not merely further transmission – through participation; that brings multiple agencies into play in ways common to performance.

Some of that variation we can only speculate about. Many polyphonic carols have fauxbourdon parts – a third vocal part that harmonizes with the other two solo voices.[64] However, this fauxbourdon part was often not written down but left to the performers to compose mentally and perform;

---

[61] R. L. Greene, ed., *The Early English Carol*, 2nd ed. (Oxford: Clarendon Press, 1977) recounts the history of the form.

[62] E.g. *A patre unigenitus* in Oxford, Bodleian Library, MS Arch. Selden B.26, f. 15r, which begins 'make we ioye nowe in this fest'. Carols are cited by the title on 'The Digital Index of Medieval English Verse', n.d., www.dimev.net.

[63] Greene, ed., *Early English Carol*, xxxii–xxxiii.

[64] E. Trumble, *Fauxbourdon: An Historical Survey* (Brooklyn: Institute of Medieval Music, 1959). J. Stevens and D. Fallows, eds., *Mediaeval Carols*, 3rd ed. (London:

creation and publication continued within the act of performing. Performance might also account for variation in the wording of carols as it recurs in different manuscripts. An example of such variation can be seen in the carol 'As I Lay upon a Night', which appears in four manuscripts (cited hereafter as Sloane, Balliol, Selden and Trinity).[65] The relatively high number of manuscripts of this carol and its structural stability suggest that it was popular, and that exemplars were easily accessible. The verse order overall is generally consistent and echoes that found in the earliest manuscript of the carol (Trinity).[66] The four manuscripts do, however, have variants, as shown in Table 1. (The archaic letters thorn and yogh have been modernized in quotations and tables.)

The main variations between these versions of 'As I Lay upon a Night' are two. One is of omission, as the Balliol manuscript omits the fifth verse. One is of addition, as the Sloane manuscript includes two additional verses (its verses four and five) in the middle of the carol. These verses recur in another popular carol, 'In Bethlehem That Fair City', which exists in six manuscripts which range in date across the fifteenth century, two of them also containing 'As I Lay upon a Night'.[67] Of these six manuscripts of 'In Bethlehem That Fair City', the additional verses of 'As I Lay upon a Night' in Sloane resemble the version in the Balliol manuscript most closely. A comparison between both carols is shown in Table 2.[68]

Stainer & Bell, 2018), transcribes musically-notated carols and includes their fauxbourdon parts.

[65] The manuscripts are London, British Library, Sloane MS 2593; Oxford, Balliol College, MS 354; Oxford, Bodleian Library, MS Arch. Selden B.26; Cambridge, Trinity College, MS O.3.58.

[66] The appearance of 'Deo Gratias Anglia (The Agincourt Carol)' in Trinity provides an earliest dating for this manuscript soon after the battle of Agincourt in 1415.

[67] 'In Bethlehem That Fair City' occurs in Balliol and Trinity, as well as Oxford, Bodleian Library, MS Eng. poet e.1; Cambridge, University Library, MS Ee.1.12; London, British Library, Additional MS 31042; and Oxford, Lincoln College, MS Lat. 141.

[68] Transcriptions are my own and compared with Greene, ed., *Early English Carols*, no. 21.A and no. 234.C. The first added verse also resembles the last in Lincoln.

Table 1 The order of verses in 'As I Lay upon a Night' across four manuscripts

Trinity	Sloane	Selden	Balliol
As I lay …	As I lay …	As y lay …	As I me lay …
To here cam Gabryel …	To here cam Gabriel …	Ther come Gabriel with lyght …	To her com an angell …
At that wurd …	After that word …	Ther she con-ceyved God almyght …	At that word …
Qwan Jhesu on the rode …	Ryght as the sunne schynit …	Whan Jhesu was on the rode ypyght …	When Jhesu on the rode …
Jhesu that syttyst …	Now is born that babe …	And after to heuen …	
	After to heuene		

The additional verses of the Sloane manuscript also occur at the same point as the verses in 'In Bethlehem That Fair City' (the fourth and fifth). This could indicate that the scribe inadvertently miscopied verses of another well-known carol as part of 'As I Lay upon a Night'. However, there seems to have been some adjustment to fit the metre of the different carol and also the refrain. The final line of the second additional verse, for example, is changed from a request to be merry to 'And therfore think me that che is'. Ending the line with *she is* creates an effective lead into the Latin refrain 'redemptoris mater' (mother of the redeemer) and thus to the burden, 'Alma redemptoris mater'. The scribes of 'As I Lay upon a Night' appear to adjust the verses from 'In Bethlehem That Fair City' for a specific performance context. This is perhaps a more liturgical or Latinate context, considering that the English lines run into the Latin so seamlessly. To understand the full verse and make sense of its story,

Table 2 Comparison of 'As I Lay upon a Night' and 'In Bethlehem That Fair City'

'As I Lay upon a Night', from Sloane	'In Bethlehem That Fair City', from Balliol
Alma redemptoris mater	To blis god bryng vs all and sum
As I lay vpon a nyght	Christe redemptor omnium
My thowt was on a mayde bryght	In bedlem in that fayer cyte
That men callyn mary of myght	A chyld was born of owr lady
Redemptoris mater	Lord and prynce that he shuld be
To here cam gabriel so bryght	A solis ortus cardine
And seyde heyl mari ful of myght	Chyldren were slayn grett plente
To be cald thu art adyght	Jhesu for the love of the
Redemptoris mater	Lett vs neuer dampned be
After that word that mayde bryght	Hostes herodes ympie
Anon conseyuyd god of myght	He was born of owr lady
And therby wyst men that che hyght	Withowt wemmb of her body
Redemptoris mater	Godes son that syttyth on hye
Ryght as the sunne schynit in glas	Jhesu saluator seculi
So Ihesu in his moder was	As the son shynyth thorow the glas
And therby wyt men that che was	So Jhesu in her body was
Redemptoris mater	To serue hym he geve vs grace
	O lux beata trinitas
Now is born that babe of blys	Now ys born owr lord Jhesus
And qwen of heuene his moder is	That mad mery all vs
And therfore think me that che is	Be all mery in thys howse
Redemptoris mater	Exvltet celum lavdibus
After to heuene he tok his flyght	
And ther he sit with his fader of myght	
With hym is crownyd that lady bryght	
Redemptoris mater	

the audience would need to understand the Latin phrase 'redemptoris mater'. If they did not, the English lines at the end of each of the additional verses would end mid-phrase. Although the scribes of 'In Bethlehem That Fair City' also make use of Latin and English lines, in a manner common for macaronic carols, the Latin phrase ending each verse is transplanted in its entirety from other liturgical contexts and is more separate from the English than in 'As I Lay upon a Night'. You do not need to understand Latin to be able to understand the rest. The rewriting to integrate languages in Sloane suggests that the inclusion of these additional verses there is not erroneous but intentional. The repurposing of verses suggest that the scribe required a longer song for a different performance context or purpose, possibly a celebration of the Annunciation.

To grasp where the agency lies in such reuses of older material, one can compare the adaptation and use of lines from other sources to the act of 'sampling' in electronic music, where a previously recorded piece is reused in a new composition, often with alteration; a similar process occurred in medieval song. Liturgical material such as hymns and psalms was part of everyday life in religious communities, and phrases from pre-existing liturgical material reappear in songs, such as the lines from 'In Bethlehem That Fair City'. The medieval memory was, according to cultural historians, well trained.[69] The digital storing of samples of music can perhaps be compared to this collective cultural memory: the scribe, composer or performer would have a wealth of textual and musical material in mind when adapting carols for specific occasions, locations, performers or patrons. The use of pre-existing Latin liturgical phrases would evoke earlier texts or songs in the mind of the listeners, which they could associate with certain rites, traditions or events and embed in the memory through performing and listening.

The impact of cultural memory and oral tradition can often be seen on the page itself. The carol 'There Is No Rose' is an example of this. This

---

[69] A. M. B. Berger, *Medieval Music and the Art of Memory* (Los Angeles: University of California Press, 2005).

carol occurs in two manuscripts: the Trinity manuscript and one now in the library at Holkham Hall. Their two texts of 'There Is No Rose' differ, as is seen in Table 3.[70] Jeremy Griffiths, who found the copy at Holkham Hall, pointed out that this scribe had trouble with copying at line divisions: he noted that 'the pattern of deleted letters

Table 3 Two versions of 'There Is No Rose'

Trinity	Holkham Hall, MS 755
[Ther is no] rose of swych vertu	Make yhow mery and do gladly
As is the rose that bare Jhesu	And ~~gh~~ glade be al thys company
[There is no rose of] swych vertu	letabundus
As is the rose that bar Jhesu	Ther is no rose of [su]che vertu ~~h~~
Alleluya	has ys the rosse that bar ~~a~~ Iehsu
For in this rose conteynyd was	alleluya
Heuen and erthe in lytyl space	In that rose conteynyd yt was
Res miranda	heuyn and herthe and lytyl spas
Be that rose we may weel see	Ros miranda
That he is God in personys thre	by that rose ye mow a se ~~þat he~~
Pari forma	that he ys gode yn personys þre
The aungelys sungyn the sheperdes to	Pare forma
Gloria in excelcis Deo	Y blessyd be schege a chylde
Gaud[e]amus	for he ys y bore bothe meke and mylde
[L]eue we al this wordly merthe	gaudiamus
And folwe we this ioyful berthe	leue we al thys worlyche mys
Transeamus	And take we al thys worlyche blys
	grasiamus

[70] Based on Greene, ed., *Early English Carols*, no. 173, and J. Griffiths, 'Unrecorded Middle English Verse in the Library at Holkham Hall, Norfolk', *Medium Aevum*, 64 (1995), 278–84 (282).

in this copy' (marked by text struck through in Table 3) suggested that 'the lines of verse were not clearly separated in the scribe's exemplar and that the separation was being undertaken by the scribe as he wrote'.[71] However, an alternative explanation for the scribe's mistakes could be that he was copying from a memory of performance instead of an exemplar. If this were so, he would have had to rely on recollecting and 'internally hearing' the performance, remembering the words but having to figure out the structure and line breaks in the process of transcription, resulting in mistakes on the page.

The burden of the 'There Is No Rose' in the Holkham copy also varies from that of the Trinity one. The Holkham version begins: 'Make yhow mery and do gladly | And ~~gh~~ glade be al thys company'. This implies a group gathered for the purpose of listening to a performance and perhaps participating by singing the burden, the 'company'. It also creates an invitation for this group to make merry. Thus this carol lends itself to an active performance. Oral tradition could, therefore, have continued to play a part in the transmission of carols. The kinds of agency in transmitting the poem and in then reshaping it are complex, some perhaps intentional, some perhaps unintentional, some from inherited tradition, some from individual scribes or would-be authors.

Through such variation, this dual process of performed publication and written publication depends on a variety of players: the composer, the scribes, performers, the intended audience, the intended performer, to name but a few. It is hard to say for sure where the agency lies in the new dissemination of prior, traditional material such as lines of Latin liturgy. If we consider the sharing of such carols as acts of publication, and not merely transmission, given that it blends writing, performance, and memory, then further questions of originality arise.

[71] Griffiths, 'Unrecorded Middle English Verse', 281.

The Limits of Agency in Athenian Inscriptions, by Edward Jones

As well as passing on traditional material, the medieval carols were reshaped by scribes and singers with particular skills in making manuscripts or performing music. Another question about the agency behind unprinted media concerns the degree to which such media are accessible and usable. It was suggested (as by Jarvis, cited earlier) that the press, with its specialized and expensive technology and susceptibility to social control, affords less agency to people than unprinted media. But most unprinted media – with perhaps the exception of simple speech – require the mastery of skills, and those skills are sometimes limited to people with a particular profession or training or some social distinction. Given those practical limits, the chance to communicate publicly is limited, or mediated, by certain groups.

A typical unprinted medium that requires specialized skills is carving into stone and other materials. There are instructive examples of how this affects who gets to address the public in some stone inscriptions from Classical Athens. With the exception of graffiti and other short inscriptions, which Robert Pitt calls 'little epigraphy', most ancient Greek inscriptions were cut by craftsmen who counted inscribing texts on stone among their talents.[72] There is no specific ancient Greek term to describe such craftsmen, though for the sake of convenience we may call these craftsmen (stone) cutters.[73] The cutter worked from a draft text provided by the commissioner, typically a private individual or an official acting on behalf of a community.[74] Unfortunately, the surviving literary texts provide little

---

[72] R. Pitt, 'Little Epigraphy: Texts on Public and Private Objects', *Lampas*, 54 (2021), 119–36.

[73] On stone cutters, see, above all, Stephen Tracy's studies: e.g. S. V. Tracy, *Athenian Lettering of the Fifth Century B.C.: The Rise of the Professional Letter Cutter* (Berlin: De Gruyter, 2016).

[74] See C. Pébarthe, *Cité, démocratie et écriture: histoire de l'alphabétisation d'Athènes à l'époque classique* (Paris: De Boccard, 2006), 247–60, and I. Berti, 'Quanto costa incidere una stele? Costi di produzione e meccanismi di pubblicazione delle iscrizioni pubbliche in Grecia', *HISTORIKA: Studi di storia greca e romana*, 3 (2014), 11–46.

commentary on the production of inscriptions. Epigraphic sources, however, shed light on the costs involved; we also possess inscribed contracts
(from non-Athenian contexts) ordering the cutter, for instance, to use
letters of a certain height.[75]

Except where the cutter needed to abbreviate words, he was bound to
follow the draft text to the letter – even abbreviations may have been
present in the draft. Thus, textual agency was the preserve of the commissioner. Decisions regarding layout were presumably guided partly by
financial considerations; inscribing in columns, rather than a single paragraph of continuous text, was more expensive, for the former layout left
valuable space uninscribed. Commissioning parties therefore logically had
some say over the format employed. So too, however, did the cutter: since
formatting was also a technical issue, he was ultimately responsible for
determining line length, including the spacing of letters. Some cutters
apparently did not even begin inscribing with a fixed layout.[76] The question
of textual and material agency is thus complex.

A loose distinction between public and private epigraphy helps to frame
the different ways in which that agency was exercised. Here, the terms
public and *private* refer respectively to inscriptions commissioned by political and civic communities (for example, a city-state), and those commissioned by individuals and smaller groups (for example, a family). Although
some private inscriptions were not intended for public consumption – for
example, curse tablets were often deliberately buried underground or
submerged in water – most were displayed in sanctuaries or cemeteries,
that is, in sacred, public space. Epitaphs (that is, funerary inscriptions) were
one common form of private inscription and were typically displayed at
cemeteries. Their texts were sometimes carved on a base carrying sculpture
in the round, or on a marble stele featuring sculpture in relief. Thus, any

---

[75] Berti, 'Quanto costa?', discusses the costs. See R. Pitt, 'Just as It Has Been
Written: Inscribing Building Contracts at Lebadeia', in N. Papazarkadas, ed. *The
Epigraphy and History of Boeotia* (Leiden: Brill, 2014), 386–91, for inscribed
contracts for cutters.

[76] S. V. Tracy, *The Lettering of an Athenian Mason* (Princeton: ASCSA, 1975), 118–20.

epitaph must be treated both as a text and monument, and any discussion of agency must also take materials and iconography into account.[77]

The dead, of course, can neither speak nor write. Some epitaphs may have been prepared by the deceased prior to their death.[78] Otherwise, they were composed afterwards, usually by relatives. Each text typically mentions the deceased's name, though besides this obvious feature their content varies. The status of the deceased, the conventional and generic language of the day and idiosyncratic taste all influenced the inscribed text. A late fifth-century BCE funerary *stele* (a tall, rectangular marble slab) for a woman, found in the Kerameikos cemetery in Athens, identifies the deceased simply as 'Hegeso of Proxenos' (Figure 2). On its own, this tells the modern reader relatively little, though a contemporary observer would know that an Athenian citizen woman was identified by her *kurios* ('guardian'), normally her father or husband.

The text was inscribed on a pediment carved in relief. Beneath the inscription are two female figures also carved in relief – the figure on the right sits on a stool, her head tilted downwards in the direction of a jewellery box held by the standing figure on the left. The iconography is that of the elite citizen woman attended by her maid, with the former performing a role appropriate to her gender and status within the *oikos* ('household'). Consequently, the figure on the right is to be identified with the 'Hegeso' of the epitaph; the text works in tandem with the relief, though it is the iconography of the latter that transforms Hegeso from a nondescript into an idealized female citizen. One cannot, however, analyze her *stele* in isolation, for it was discovered in situ alongside two or three additional

---

[77] Compared with funerary inscriptions or dedicatory inscriptions, public inscriptions were less frequently decorated with sculpture. However, see C. L. Lawton, *Attic Document Reliefs: Art and Politics in Ancient Athens* (Oxford: Clarendon Press, 1995).

[78] Pre-mortem composition possibly underlies *IG* II^2 5673, a mid-fourth century BCE funerary inscription for two sisters from Piraeus. Its text was inscribed at the same time, and it has been suggested that this occurred between the deaths of the sisters: see K. Backler, 'Sisterhood, Affection and Enslavement in Hyperides' *Against Timandrus*', *Classical Quarterly*, 72.2 (2022), 469–86 (475–6).

Figure 2 Grave stele of Hegeso (*c.* 410–400 BCE), National Archaeological Museum (NAMA 3624), Athens. © Vicenç Valcárcel Pérez / Wikimedia Commons / CC-BY-SA-4.0

funerary *stelai* of a specific family, which were displayed together in a *peribolos* tomb (a grave enclosure). Since they do not mention his name, Proxenos is accordingly to be identified as Hegeso's father; Hegeso was presumably married to one of the men commemorated at the tomb.[79] The grouping and positioning of these funerary monuments create what one scholar has described as 'a symbolic portrait of this citizen family, together in death as they were in life'.[80] The extent to which Hegeso herself played a part in constructing this 'portrait' is unclear. If its text and relief were pre-planned, she may have had a say over her monument's final form. But the interpretation of her *stele* and adjacent *stelai* is further complicated by modern uncertainty about their chronological sequence.[81] As is often the case, the different agencies implicated in Hegeso's monument are elusive.

In some instances, epitaphs contain what appears to be first-person speech. For example, in a metrical text inscribed on the front face of a base dating circa 550–530 BCE, we read: 'I, Phrasikleia's grave marker, shall always be called girl (*koure*), having received this name from the gods instead of marriage.' On a lateral face, we read 'Aristion of Paros made me'. Atop the base stands the fruit of Aristion's labour, a marble *kore* ('girl' or 'maiden') – a sculpture depicting a young female figure (Figure 3).

The dedication of *korai* (plural of *kore*) was a common practice on the Acropolis during this period. Less common were specifically funerary *korai* such as Phrasikleia's. Like marble *kouroi* (sculptures depicting male figures), *korai* do not bear anatomically distinctive features. Scholars have therefore identified these female figures variously, as representations of Athena, as priestesses, as participants in ritual, or as generic, anonymous and idealized representations of citizen women.[82] In Phrasikleia's case, it is probable but

[79] R. Garland, '*A First Catalogue of Attic Peribolos Tombs*', Annual of the British School at Athens, 77 (1982), 142, A20.

[80] A. F. Stewart, *Art, Desire, and the Body in Ancient Greece* (Cambridge: Cambridge University Press, 1998), 124.

[81] S. C. Humphreys, *Kinship in Ancient Athens: An Anthropological Analysis* (Oxford: Oxford University Press, 2019), 367–8.

[82] On *korai*, see M. Stieber, *The Poetics of Appearance in the Attic Korai* (Austin: University of Texas Press, 2004); cf. C. Keesling, *The Votive Statues of the Athenian Acropolis* (Cambridge: Cambridge University Press, 2008).

Figure 3 Funerary monument for Phrasikleia (*c.* 550–450 BCE), National Archaeological Museum (NAMA 4889), Athens. © User:Sailko / Wikimedia Commons / CC-BY-SA-3.0.

not certain that the *kore* represents a maiden (i.e. an unmarried female figure), whether generic or mythological (Persephone being the archetypal mythical *kore*). The sculpture represents the visual foil to the aural message of the inscription: the textual-material ensemble ensured that Phrasikleia was both known and seen as a maiden. Did Phrasikleia herself compose the text, cognizant of her impending demise? In the absence of firm evidence, this seems improbable. Phrasikleia's is not the only example of a grave marker or object that speaks in the first person.[83] It is perhaps preferable to view the 'I' of her inscription not as a stark expression of female agency in a deeply patriarchal society but as an attempt by its author or authors (presumably one or more of her relatives) to imbue the monument with 'agency' in the sense that Alfred Gell used the term.[84] In the Phrasikleia inscription, the first person renders the inanimate animate; it is Phrasikleia's grave marker, and not Phrasikleia herself, that speaks.

We turn now from private to public inscriptions, such as laws, lists and accounts, which were set up in what we would call public spaces, for example, an agora (a meeting place or market), or in simultaneously sacred and public spaces like sanctuaries. In Classical Athens many inscribed decrees passed by the assembly were erected on the Acropolis, the most sacred area of this city-state.[85] Like other ancient Greek communities, the Athenians did not recognise a distinction between 'church' and 'state'; religious activity was a distinctly public, collective affair, and many inscribed laws displayed at sanctuaries concerned sacred matters.[86] Scholars have sometimes argued that this choice of display was intended to grant the legislation divine protection or legitimacy. The invocation or recognition of divine agency is detectable in the inscription of 'Gods', or a similar superscript, above the first line of some public inscriptions. While

---

[83] On 'speaking objects', including inscriptions, see M. Burzachechi, 'Oggetti parlanti nelle epigrafi greche', *Epigraphica: Rivista italiana di Epigrafia*, 24 (1962), 3–54; J. Svenbro, *Phrasikleia: An Anthropology of Reading in Ancient Greece*, trans. J. Lloyd (Ithaca, NY: Cornell University Press, 1993), 8–43; J. Whitley, 'Why με? Personhood and Agency in the Earliest Greek Inscriptions', in P. J. Boyes, P. M. Steele, and N. Elvira Astoreca, eds. *The Social and Cultural Contexts of Historic Writing Practices*, vol. 2 (Oxford: Oxbow, 2021), 269–87 (especially 273–6).

[84] A. Gell, *Art and Agency* (Oxford: Clarendon, 1998); Whitley, 'Why με?', 271–3.

[85] P. Liddel, 'The Places of Publication of Athenian State Decrees from the 5th Century BC to the 3rd Century AD', *Zeitschrift für Papyrologie und Epigraphik*, 143 (2003), 79–93. The Acropolis summit was home to the cult of Athena Polias (Athens' patron deity).

[86] R. Parker, *Polytheism and Society in Ancient Athens* (Oxford: Oxford University Press, 2005), 90–1.

no ancient source comments on these superscripts, their authors apparently envisaged some kind of involvement for the gods.[87] Such imagining of non-human agency for texts is not as outlandish as it might sound; in twenty-first-century journalism, people make similar ascriptions of agency to powers other than the human, now to artificial intelligence (as is shown in the next section).

Whereas private inscriptions were authored by individuals or families, public inscriptions were drawn up by collectives, for example, the male citizen body, or smaller groups such as the deme (a civic subdivision of the Athenian city-state, somewhat akin to the parish). At a basic level, then, public inscriptions expressed collective agency. An explicit expression of this agency can be seen in inscribed decrees (that is, those enacted by the citizen body), which typically begin with the declaration that 'it was decided by the council and the people'. In this formula, the 'people' (*demos*) refers to the male citizens assembled on the Pnyx, the hill west of the Acropolis where the Athenians voted on legislation. These decrees were enacted by a section rather than the whole of the male citizen body, for not every member of the *demos* could be in attendance. Furthermore, legislation was proposed by individuals, who were mentioned in the preamble of decrees, and official secretaries – in Athens, the council's secretary – were responsible for having the text of the decree inscribed. Inscribed versions of decrees sometimes lack requisite publication formulae, such as a clause authorizing the inscription of the stone version and its erection in public space.[88] Yet secretaries were not permitted to add and erase as they saw fit, and it is probably best to view such discrepancies as accidental and banal rather than intentional and ideological. Whereas in Athens inscribed decrees were enacted in the name of the people and erected in prominent space (the Acropolis), laws and rules instituted by other communities expressed narrower forms of authority, and were often much less accessible (as, for example, were rules in the monasteries of thirteenth-century Tibet (see Chapter 3).

[87] W. Mack, 'Vox Populi, Vox Deorum? Athenian Document Reliefs and the Theologies of Public Inscription', *Annual of the British School at Athens*, 113 (2018), 365–98.

[88] R. Osborne, *Athens and Athenian Democracy* (Cambridge: Cambridge University Press, 2010), 64–82.

Although there was sometimes a gap between the precise content of a given legal text and the inscribed version of that text, the Athenians, and more broadly the Greeks, treated the inscribed version as authoritative. This is significant: scholars debate the extent to which Greek communities stored and retained documents recorded on perishable media like papyrus, though it is clear that not all legislation was inscribed on stone.[89] Even if we allow that perishable copies of legislation were retained and consulted at something approaching an archive, the habit of treating *stelai* as authoritative texts nevertheless demonstrates the agency exerted by permanent, stone inscriptions. That agency is also visible in the erasure and re-inscription of certain clauses in inscribed decrees. For example, a late fifth-century BCE Athenian decree ordered a secretary to erase and reinscribe part of an earlier decree so that it no longer referred to Neapolis, the object of its attention and praise, as a 'colony of the Thasians'.[90] Situated on the mainland roughly opposite the island of Thasos, Neapolis had by this time achieved significant independence from its mother city. The colonial link was accordingly eschewed. While epigraphic publication was typically final and literally monolithic, and should therefore be distinguished from performance qua publication (as in the medieval carols in the previous section), there were occasionally opportunities to revise the inscribed text.

Finally, let us consider another type of public inscription, the 'inscribed account' – an umbrella term for inscribed accounts of money, inventories of sacred or public property, sales of property or leases, and so on. Inscribed accounts typically contain a heading mentioning a board of officials who were responsible for the transactions recorded in the text of the account proper. For example, an account from 367/6 BCE features a heading announcing that 'the *poletai* (state auctioneers) ... sold the following', and then provides records of the sale of confiscated property and, separately, mining leases.[91] Although officials appear in the headings of inscribed

[89] P. J. Rhodes, 'Public Documents in the Greek States: Archives and Inscriptions', *Greece and Rome*, 48 (2001), 33–44, 136–53.

[90] R. Osborne and P. J. Rhodes, eds., *Greek Historical Inscriptions: 478–404 BC* (Oxford: Oxford University Press, 2017), no. 187, ll. 58–9.

[91] P. J. Rhodes and R. Osborne, eds., *Greek Historical Inscriptions: 404–323 BC* (Oxford: Oxford University Press, 2003), no. 36, ll. 1–8.

accounts, a decree (enacted by the council and the people) authorized their inscription. Officials were also seemingly instructed to include certain categories of information in the inscriptions. This institutional arrangement did not, however, prevent officials from shaping the accounts' final form and content. For example, they were apparently left to decide how best to compose introductory headings or to format the text.

The processes that led to the publication of an inscribed account therefore channelled both the collective agency of the Athenian people and the narrower agency of the officials themselves. This balance ought to be considered when assessing the function of such inscriptions: the officials responsible for inscribing a given account potentially saw the resulting inscription as a commemorative monument or quasi-legal document, whereas the *demos* perhaps viewed that same inscription as a symbol of their power to command officials, as a publicly available source of information or (with reference to inventories of sacred treasure) as an expression of the community's piety – or all of the above.[92]

To draw sharp conclusions from the analysis of a small number of inscriptions, let alone only those discovered in Attica, would be unwise. However, it is clear that different entanglements of agency underpinned the production of different kinds of inscriptions. At a basic level, the distinction between private and public epigraphy can be understood as a distinction between individual and collective agency. But we have seen that even funerary monuments – inscriptions that ostensibly articulated an acutely individual mode of agency – were shaped by potentially complex sets of social relations. An epitaph recording the death of an individual therefore cannot be regarded merely as an expression of individual agency. With reference to public inscriptions, inscribed laws were not simply monuments authored and set up by 'the people', since other agents – individual proposers, secretaries, and sometimes even the gods – were involved in their creation and message. Similarly, an inscribed account was both a product of collective agency and that of the officials tasked with creating it.

---

[92] Scholars debate the function of inscribed accounts: see J. K. Davies, 'Accounts and Accountability in Classical Athens', in R. Osborne and S. Hornblower, eds., *Ritual, Finance, Politics: Athenian Democratic Accounts* (Oxford: Clarendon Press, 1994), 201–12.

AI and Agency in Journalism, by Felix M. Simon

For writing in the public record in the twenty-first century, digital technologies might seem to escape the constraints of traditional content and technical skill that other media – manuscript, liturgy or inscription as much as print – brought. Social media seem like the ultimate exercise of agency by a wide community of people in publishing their opinions and images, but they depend on the work of others who created and curated the platforms which that community uses. Likewise, the use of artificial intelligence (AI) is now changing the mediation of agency and therefore conditions of publishing. One sphere in which some of those consequential changes can be observed is news and journalism. How has the agency in news publishing been changed by AI?

To answer this question, let's first go back to the definition of *publication* and *publishing*. It relates to producing something that is in some shape and form meant to be public – seen, perceived and consumed by more than just the author (which distinguishes it from mere writing or creating). It is also an active endeavour, carried out by one or more agents, at least one of which has an intention of some kind. Journalism, the process of making the news and producing reality instead of fictional media, is one such act of publication. Producing the 'news' (a specific item of information that has value as recent or previously unknown information) is an active process by agents, usually journalists, with at least one intention: creating something to be seen by a public. One does not even have to look particularly closely to identify multiple intentions of journalistic 'agents' in this minimalist definition of journalism (striving for accuracy, or timeliness, for example).

One of the inherent historic tensions in journalism is between individualistic agency and autonomy – a journalist's capacity to act in a self-directing manner – on the one hand, and the political, economic, organizational, technological and professional conditions that constrain the same on the other. In other words, while journalists like to think that they work free from constraints, journalistic agency is always already bounded. It is hemmed in by the political environment (e.g. reporting from or in an authoritarian state is not the same as from a liberal democratic one), the economic and organizational circumstances (e.g. pursuing investigative reporting is easier at a well-off news organization than in precarious conditions), technological configurations (e.g. a modern content management system (CMS) makes life easier than an old one) and finally the professional and legal codes which to some extent dictate how the journalists ought to do and can do their work.[93] These structures have historically held primacy over the agency and autonomy of most journalists.

The dawn of the digital age has added further complexity, mostly by elevating the importance of one of these factors: technology. Since the 1990s, news publishing and journalism have become increasingly shaped by a large technological system of digital media, composed of various decision-making non-human entities.[94] Among these entities one finds the algorithms and recommendation systems that, on the one hand, help journalists find stories and process information and, on the other hand, shape how the finished product of journalism – the news – reaches audiences, both through publishers' own infrastructures and products and the communication infrastructures that enable and sustain the public arena.[95]

The latest iteration in this development is the increasing use of artificial intelligence (AI) in journalism and the news. While the definition of AI and the usefulness of the term remain contested,[96] most experts agree that it does not encompass conscious, general intelligence (so-called AGI) that rivals

[93] P. J. Shoemaker and S. D. Reese, *Mediating the Message in the 21st Century: A Media Sociology Perspective* (New York: Routledge, 2013).

[94] See T. P. Hughes, 'The Evolution of Large Technological Systems', in W. E. Bijker, T. P. Hughes, and T. Pinch, eds., *The Social Construction of Technological Systems* (Cambridge, MA: MIT Press, 2012), 45–76; A. Jungherr, G. Rivero, and D. Gayo-Avello, *Retooling Politics: How Digital Media Are Shaping Democracy* (Cambridge: Cambridge University Press, 2020).

[95] A. Jungherr and R. Schroeder, *Digital Transformations of the Public Arena* (Cambridge: Cambridge University Press, 2021).

[96] M. H. Jarrahi, C. Lutz, and G. Newlands, 'Artificial Intelligence, Human Intelligence and Hybrid Intelligence Based on Mutual Augmentation', *Big Data and Society*, 9 (2022); S. Cave, 'The Problem with Intelligence: Its Value-Laden History and the Future of AI', in *Proceedings of the AAAI/ACM Conference on AI, Ethics, and Society* (New York: ACM, 2020), 29–35.

and surpasses human intelligence in all domains.[97] Within the news industry, AI at the time of writing is used to refer to 'narrow' computer systems using machine learning (ML) approaches and to forms of generative AI, that is, computer systems capable of producing new forms of data such as realistic texts and images. These systems learn from data and feedback through algorithms trained on large datasets, gradually improving their performance on specific tasks over time.

AI is employed both in the production of news, for example to write or augment texts, and in the distribution of news, for example to tailor content to users' interests or to automate parts of the distribution process.[98] In 2023, the most recent and most advanced form of AI used in news organizations and beyond were so-called Large Language Models (LLMs). But what are they exactly? We put this question to OpenAI's ChatGPT (version 3.5) using the following prompt in July 2023:

```
Define what an LLM is in three short sentences.
```

We received an answer that instead defines the 'LLM' graduate degree in law! But we posed the same question to Google's BARD and received the following reply:

```
Sure, here is a definition of LLM in three short
sentences:
```

- A large language model (LLM) is a type of artificial intelligence (AI) that can process and generate human language.
- LLMs are trained on massive datasets of text and code, which allows them to learn the statistical relationships between words and phrases.

---

[97] M. Mitchell, *Artificial Intelligence: A Guide for Thinking Humans* (London: Pelican, 2019).

[98] For an overview, see e.g. F. M. Simon, 'Artificial Intelligence in the News. How AI Retools, Rationalizes, and Reshapes Journalism and the Public Arena' (New York, NY: Tow Center for Digital Journalism, January 2024), www.cjr .org/tow_center_reports/artificial-intelligence-in-the-news.php.

- LLMs can be used for a variety of tasks, including translation, summarization, and question answering.

Now, that's more like it. What already becomes apparent is that these models do not think (to the best of our knowledge) or understand. Instead, after being trained on very large datasets, they generate a vast, tokenized vocabulary that predicts word sequence probabilities and outputs natural language.[99] While BARD took into account more up-to-date information and reflects the fact that the abbreviation LLM is now commonly used in the context of AI-systems, ChatGPT 3.5 worked on older training data, according to which it was indeed more likely that a user would be interested in the definition of a Master of Laws degree.

Many of these complex computer systems can handle multiple language-related tasks (e.g. text-generation, translation), while others are multi-modal – capable of processing and generating realistic-appearing videos, images and audio in addition to text. In contrast to AI systems for single tasks, they are significantly broader in the ways they can be used and in the things they can do – in other words, their affordances.[100] One of these is the ability to communicate in a human-like fashion.[101] They answer as a human would and are interacted with in the same way. This affordance not only makes them more accessible, it also explains their popularity.

Now what has this short digression into Large Language Models and chatbots got to do with journalism? Let's go to ChatGPT again for an answer, using the following prompt:

[99] S. Wolfram, 'What Is ChatGPT Doing . . . and Why Does It Work?', Stephen Wolfram, 14 February 2023, https://writings.stephenwolfram.com/2023/02/what-is-chatgpt-doing-and-why-does-it-work/.

[100] S. K. Evans et al., 'Explicating Affordances: A Conceptual Framework for Understanding Affordances in Communication Research', *Journal of Computer-Mediated Communication*, 22 (2017), 35–52 (36).

[101] S. C. Lewis and F. M. Simon, 'Why Human-Machine Communication Matters for the Study of Artificial Intelligence in Journalism', in A. L. Guzman, R. McEwen, and S. Jones, eds., *The SAGE Handbook of Human-Machine Communication* (New York: SAGE, 2023), 516–23.

Imagine you are a journalist and good at researching content. Your task is to turn these bullet points based on my error-riddled notes into a paragraph of about 50 words. Copy-edit the text. Style: British English.

- AI more entrenched in news work, central in how journalists do jobs.
- This matters. Addresses the question of this section in book: How has AI changed agency and therefore publishing?
- My argument: AI shapes and limits the agency of journalists, and their autonomy. Reinforces tensions mentioned earlier, between individualistic agency and autonomy – a journalists' capacity to act (agency) in a self-directing manner (autonomy) – on the one hand, and the conditions that constrain the same, with a focus on the technological conditions.

This was ChatGPT's unedited answer:

AI has increasingly become deeply ingrained in the field of news, transforming the way journalists carry out their work. The implications of this development are crucial as they address the core question explored in this section of the book: How has AI altered the concept of agency and, consequently, publishing? In the forthcoming argument, it will be posited that AI systems, particularly chatbots like ChatGPT, possess the ability to shape and restrict the agency and autonomy of journalists. This is primarily due to their capacity to simulate human-like communication and capabilities. As a result, the tensions within journalism, previously mentioned, between individualistic agency and autonomy on one hand, and the constraining conditions, particularly those driven by technology, on the other hand, are further accentuated. Ultimately, this reshapes the landscape

of journalism publishing in unprecedented and
noteworthy ways.

With a few strokes on my keyboard, I have turned an AI system trained in human-like communication into something of a journalistic research assistant and copy-editor. It has taken a few error-riddled notes, and has turned them into a transition paragraph for this text, at the same time demonstrating the point I am trying to make here.

One way we can read the ongoing AI debate, along with the apprehensions voiced by journalists, artists and other 'content creators,' is by viewing it as a story of these groups striving to safeguard their agency and autonomy in the face of technologies that are perceived as particularly threatening in this respect. Consequently, the impact of AI on journalism and publishing extends beyond mere improvements in efficiency or the enhancement of human labour. It becomes a tale of journalists interrogating, negotiating and safeguarding not only their roles in contemporary news organizations but also the integrity of their journalistic practices on a broader scale.

The influence of 'narrow' AI systems on journalists' autonomy and agency is already evident in various ways. For instance, the implementation of machine-learning systems that assist editors in deciding whether to place an article behind a paywall, as seen at the German newspaper *Frankfurter Allgemeine Zeitung*, presents a subtle limitation of their agency and autonomy, despite its facilitative role and the ability for manual override.[102] Similarly, the use of transcription software, although voluntary and resulting in significant efficiency gains, still restricts journalists' autonomy and agency, for example by potentially introducing errors or omitting contextual nuances that would have been captured by a human transcriber. However, the clearest cases can be found in the realm of chatbots.

---

[102] G. Rabenstein, 'Using AI to Predict What Should Go behind a Paywall', Google, 8 June 2021, https://blog.google/outreach-initiatives/google-news-initiative/using-ai-predict-what-should-go-behind-paywall/.

Whether chatbots or certain AI systems possess their own agency is a contested question, and the answer depends on which philosophical camp one subscribes to. The standard theory of agency explains it in terms of an agent's 'desires, beliefs, and intentions'.[103] There is disagreement among experts about whether large language models and chatbots 'understand',[104] whether they have an internal model of the world or intentions. The current consensus seems to be that this is not the case and that these models merely 'create things which look like things in their training sets',[105] lacking representational mental states and consciousness. This, then, would rule out the idea that they have true agency, at least in the narrow sense.

We can, however, side-step the thorny question of whether these AI systems have true agency by focusing on two things. First, humans by and large already treat them *as if* they have some form of agency, because we find it hard not to anthropomorphize them (as with the 'speaking' inscriptions of Athens in the previous section). There are, by now, countless stories of humans trusting their output for various important decisions, including court cases.[106] Second, if one takes the broadest possible definition of agency at face value – that agency occurs wherever 'entities enter into causal relationships, ... act on each other and interact with each other, bringing about changes in each other' – [107] then we are confronted with a neat description of what these systems do. Even if they have no true agency of their own (something we will perhaps never know), they are treated as if they had some agency, mostly because they are able to reproduce 'not the intelligence of people but the informativity of

---

[103] M. Schlosser, 'Agency', in E. N. Zalta, ed. *The Stanford Encyclopedia of Philosophy* (Stanford, CA: Metaphysics Research Lab, 2019), https://plato.stanford.edu/archives/win2019/entries/agency/.

[104] A. Tamkin et al., 'Understanding the Capabilities, Limitations, and Societal Impact of Large Language Models', arXiv, 4 February 2021, http://arxiv.org/abs/2102.02503.

[105] L. Siegele, 'How AI Could Change Computing, Culture and the Course of History', *The Economist*, 20 April 2023.

[106] D. Milmo, 'Two US Lawyers Fined for Submitting Fake Court Citations from ChatGPT', *The Guardian*, 23 June 2023.

[107] Schlosser, 'Agency'.

communication', in the words of the sociologist Elena Esposito.[108] And as technological systems they act in the world, are embedded in causal relationships with journalists, but also increasingly audiences, and bring about changes in what these agents do – if only by improving their copy (as in our example). They exhibit limited agency and condition the agency of others.

For journalistic agency and the ways in which it is reshaped by AI, this matters in two ways. In some cases, AI can augment journalists' agency, enhancing their capacity to act. The analysis of large data leaks for potential stories, for example, would not be possible without machine-learning approaches. Speeding up dull tasks, such as re-formatting content for different distribution channels – online story to tweet, tweet to TikTok reel – can be empowering. Yet, the flipside is that these systems limit journalists' discretionary decision-making ability and therefore their agency and autonomy. Where a journalist relies on, for example, a chatbot to summarize content at scale, important details may get lost or twisted out of context. Automatic translations or transcriptions can end up being riddled with errors. With LLMs this extends further, for example when they make up facts – a common feature of current systems – or introduce other people's ideas and worldviews into their output, potentially without a journalist realizing that this is happening. They might not think or understand, nor do they have politics, views or intentions of their own, but these are not prerequisites for the curtailment of journalistic agency. It is enough that these systems mirror worldviews and logics that exist in society itself – represented and reinforced through the data and methods they are trained with – and affect the routines of journalistic work by becoming part of it.

Why does it matter that journalistic publishing and journalistic agency change through a technology such as AI? The answer is found in the political and social function that journalism ideally serves: co-facilitating an informed and engaged society and an information environment that contributes to the same. Journalism is meant to be seen by a public and

---

[108] E. Esposito, *Artificial Communication: How Algorithms Produce Social Intelligence* (Cambridge, MA: MIT Press, 2022), 22.

provide this public with 'relatively accurate, accessible, diverse, relevant, and timely independently produced information about public affairs',[109] upon which they can base important decisions about their lives. It also facilitates public deliberation and as such confers power. News organizations are a central component of the public sphere, an arena that is marked by limited attention, where only so many actors and issues can be heard at the same time. News media, through journalism, play an important role as gate-keepers and often set the agenda. They can amplify and confer legitimacy on what they report on, thus empowering some and disempowering others. The exact role AI will play in this is still unclear; that it will play a role, however, is beyond doubt.

[109] R. K. Nielsen, 'The One Thing Journalism Just Might Do for Democracy', *Journalism Studies*, 18 (2017), 1251–62.

3 Public and Private Spheres

A crucial component to seeing unprinted media as vehicles for publication is recognizing the ways that these media address a wider public. With digital media or inscriptions in the landscape, that wide address seems clear (to take two examples in the previous section). But some of the Athenian inscriptions brought into public places familial records that might seem more private – depending on conceptions of privacy which change over time; and with carols or liturgical texts it is not always clear who the audience for the performance is: it could be something more like a private community, in a particular religious institution singing to itself its own variation on a carol, say, than a wider public.

That might seem problematic if a crucial component of publishing is the need to address the public. That idea does, though, seem one inherited from a myth about print, which is challenged by the particular instances gathered here. There is a prevalent, longstanding idea (influentially expressed by Benedict Anderson) that printing facilitated a community of readers who could function as a 'public sphere' or even a national public – that is, that 'Print made publics'.[110] The idea of reaching a wider public – though not a pan-historical public sphere or nation – has supported many excellent studies of past forms of media that might be considered as 'publishing'. Leah Tether has argued that 'it surely is legitimate to speak of a publishing trade prior to print' in medieval French manuscripts, in part because of 'an upsurge in the specifically commercial scope' of making manuscripts, long before printing.[111] Such accounts set the groundwork for our examination of the wide variety of media – speech and performed poetry, inscriptions and other displayed texts – used to make works for 'public consumption', as Tether helpfully puts it.[112] One could extend the list even further. In some cultures, for instance, unprinted documents sent to individual citizens were central to the creation of public authority; in others, radio was the crucial vehicle for sharing literary works across an empire.[113]

---

[110] Quoting Jarvis, *Gutenberg Parenthesis*, 14. See e.g. B. Anderson, *Imagined Communities: Reflections on the Origins and Spread of Nationalism*, rev. ed. (London: Verso, 1991).

[111] Tether, *Publishing the Grail*, 16. [112] Tether, *Publishing the Grail*, 17.

[113] E.g. respectively M. Rustow, *The Lost Archive: Traces of a Caliphate in a Cairo Synagogue* (Princeton: Princeton University Press, 2020); D. R. Morse, *Radio*

But one puzzle that emerges from our case studies (in this third chapter) is that many writers – to say nothing of people using oral media – did not necessarily seek a 'public' that was wide. They addressed smaller publics (albeit sometimes powerful ones, as with one treatise in early modern England discussed shortly), even counterpublics, and did not seek or achieve wide dissemination to a national or commercial public. This has been suggested for printing too, in recent work that has argued that the 'public sphere' was in fact multiple separate 'publics' in print – and on the internet alike.[114] So in this chapter, we not only expand our notion of what counts as publishing to cover unprinted media; we also expand – or in practice contract – the kinds of public that are addressed. Can we extend the idea of publication to 'imagined communities' on a smaller scale? Examples might include some modernist works that circulated among coteries of initiates (mentioned in our case study of Samuel Beckett), or religious ideas that came from books but spread by word of mouth among the 'interpretive communities' of illiterate people in medieval European religious groups (and in Syriac and Tibetan religious communities in case studies discussed shortly).[115] Might these small groups be thought of as 'publics', just as much as subjects of a state receiving official documents or the colonial audience of a metropolitan radio station? Even addressing a small group might be useful or meaningful for those involved; it might feel 'public' enough. And the public, however large or small, can change over time, whether by the changing intentions and agency of the makers and disseminators of the text, or in ways unforeseen by them. (One reading public now for the funerary inscriptions from Athens is classical scholars – and you, reading about them here.)

Empire: The BBC's Eastern Service and the Emergence of the Global Anglophone Novel (New York: Columbia University Press, 2020).

[114] Jarvis, *Gutenberg Parenthesis*, 154–5, 191–2.

[115] See respectively M. A. Taylor, 'Outside Joke: Virginia Woolf's Freshwater and Coterie Insularity', *Modernist Cultures*, 18 (2023), 241–60; B. Stock, *The Implications of Literacy* (Princeton: Princeton University Press, 1983).

Public and Private Spheres at Saffron Monastery, by Rosie Maxton

Some makers of unprinted media seem consciously to have envisaged – whatever they actually achieved – a wider public for their work. Even people who ostensibly address small groups can imagine that readership as part of a public that extends much further (as with the treatise on the English royal succession discussed in the next section). Yet that wider public might still be delimited by various aspects of identity. A useful demonstration of this is a manuscript produced in what might seem a closed religious community, as some of those of the medieval English carols might have been (see Chapter 2), but whose makers envisaged an audience beyond a clerical elite, defined yet still in other ways by confessional and linguistic identities. This is Dayr Zaʿfarān MS 397, an ornate lectionary of readings from the Christian Gospels.[116] It was produced in 1728 at Mor Hananyo Monastery, known colloquially as Dayr Zaʿfarān (in English, 'Saffron Monastery'). The monastery is situated just outside Mardin, a city in present-day southeast Turkey and formerly part of the eastern Ottoman Empire. Spanning nearly 700 pages, MS 397 is visually captivating: its silver cover is engraved with a scene of Christ's Passion, framed by depictions of the Virgin Mary, the apostles and the angels, and a panel of intricate geometric patterns in red and black ink adorns its title pages. Its contents are arranged in two neatly bordered columns, with the right-hand side in the Syriac language, and the left-hand in Arabic Karshuni translation ('Karshuni' refers to the transcription of non-Syriac languages in Syriac letters). By manuscript standards, it is a sumptuous and painstaking piece of work (Figure 4).

Despite being handwritten, MS 397 was created and endured as an expression of public authority. This public is, however, not to be understood as all subjects of the Ottoman realm, but rather the public that the manuscript itself delineates: namely, the Syriac Orthodox

---

[116] Mardin, Dayr Zaʿfarān, MS 397. Digital version consulted on the 'Hill Museum and Manuscript Library (HMML) Virtual Reading Room, Project No. ZFRN 00397', https://w3id.org/vhmml/readingRoom/view/208417. Hereafter ZFRN 397.

community residing within the Ottoman territories, headed by their patriarch. In particular, paratextual notes added to the main text of MS 397 – such as the scribal colophon and endowment notices – provide us with crucial information about the creation and usage of this lectionary.

Saffron Monastery had been the headquarters of the Syriac Orthodox patriarchate of Antioch since the twelfth century. Formed after the Council of Chalcedon in 451, the Syriac Orthodox Church is an Eastern Christian denomination with Syriac as its official language. Its adherents were traditionally based in Upper Mesopotamia – equating to present-day southeast Turkey, northeast Syria and northwest Iraq.[117] At the time when MS 397 was produced, however, the Syriac Orthodox were one of a rich patchwork of religious communities (including Muslims, Jews, Yazidis and Christians of other denominations) dwelling in the Ottoman Empire. This empire stretched across most of the Middle East and to parts of Eastern Europe, North Africa and Central Asia.

Although printing presses were not entirely unknown in eighteenth-century Ottoman society, hand-copied manuscripts – in Arabic, Turkish, Syriac and the myriad other languages used in the empire – were the dominant method of textual production.[118] This situation would prevail until the late nineteenth century, when print publication accelerated.[119] While book historians traditionally equated this with a slower momentum

---

[117] For an introduction to the Syriac Orthodox Church, see V. L. Menze, *Justinian and the Making of the Syrian Orthodox Church* (Oxford: Oxford University Press, 2008), esp. chapters 1 and 4.

[118] For early Ottoman printing, see e.g. I. Feodorov, *Arabic Printing for the Christians in Ottoman Lands: The East-European Connection* (Berlin: De Gruyter, 2023); V. Erginbaş, 'Enlightenment in the Ottoman Context: Ibrahim Müteferrika and his Intellectual Landscape', in G. Roper, ed. *Historical Aspects of Printing and Publishing in Languages of the Middle East* (Leiden: Brill, 2013), 53–100.

[119] A. Ayalon, *The Arabic Print Revolution: Cultural Production and Mass Readership* (Cambridge: Cambridge University Press, 2016), esp. chapter 1.

Figure 4 Mardin, Dayr Zaʿfarān, MS 397 (HMML Pr. No. ZFRN 00397), decorative front cover. Image courtesy of the Dayr Zaʿfarān (Monastery) Mardin, Turkey, and the Hill Museum & Manuscript Library. Published with permission of the owners. All rights reserved.

of social progress in comparison to Western societies, recent research is challenging this Eurocentric cast of thought.[120] In fact, as some have argued, manuscript culture better served the social and intellectual milieux of early modern Ottoman localities.[121] Moreover, even with the proliferation of the press in the nineteenth century, scribal practices continued to have a strong influence on printed materials.[122] When considering how a manuscript such as MS 397 could bear public authority, understanding the value of scribal production in the eighteenth-century Ottoman context is therefore crucial.

Public authority is particularly evoked in the scribal colophon and endowment notices found in MS 397. More than simply formulaic prose, these types of paratextual notes are increasingly being recognized in scholarship as distinct historical and social testimonies.[123] Following the biblical readings in MS 397, the scribal colophon is marked out in red, blue and gold ink. We are informed that the manuscript was copied at Saffron Monastery in the year 1728 by a monk named ʿAbd al-Nūr of Amid (Diyarbakır).[124] The scribe then acknowledges the jurisdictional framework in which the manuscript was created – a common practice

---

[120] K. A. Schwartz, 'Book History, Print, and the Middle East', *History Compass*, 15 (2017), https://doi.org/10.1111/hic3.12434; K. A. Schwartz, 'Did Ottoman Sultans Ban Print?', *Book History*, 20 (2017), 1–39.

[121] A. El Shamsy, *Rediscovering the Islamic Classics: How Editors and Print Culture Transformed an Intellectual Tradition* (Princeton: Princeton University Press, 2020), 64–65.

[122] El Shamsy, *Rediscovering the Islamic Classics*, 79–91.

[123] E.g. A. Görke and K. Hirschler, *Manuscript Notes as Documentary Sources* (Beirut: Orient-Institut, 2011), 109–32; F. Krimsti, 'Signatures of Authority: Colophons in Seventeenth-Century Melkite Circles in Aleppo', in C. D. Bahl and Stefan Hanß, eds., *Scribal Practice and the Global Cultures of Colophons, 1400–1800* (Basingstoke: Palgrave Macmillan, 2022), 109–32; H. L. Murre-van den Berg, *Scribes and Scriptures: The Church of the East in the Eastern Ottoman Provinces (1500–1850)* (Leuven: Peeters, 2015), 7–8, and chapter 3.

[124] ZFRN 397, p. 679, c. 1.

in Syriac manuscripts.[125] He records that it was copied in the days of Patriarch Ignatius Shukr Allāh II (1722–1745), leader of the Syriac Orthodox community. After the patriarch follows a complete list of the church hierarchy, comprising twenty metropolitans and bishops, occupying sees from Mardin to Aleppo to Jerusalem to Mosul to Baghdad.[126]

The scribe then identifies the commissioner of the manuscript as none other than the patriarch:

> He [Patriarch Shukr Allāh] took care of the cost of this holy book, and at his order we translated all that was Syriac in the [original] text into the Arabic language, leaving no section untranslated. This was at his bidding for public benefit (*manfaʿat al-ʿām*), readers and listeners [alike], and he made this noble book a perpetual endowment to Saffron Monastery, the patriarchal seat.[127]

The colophon establishes the authority of the manuscript both by recalling the extended hierarchy of the Syriac Orthodox Church, and connecting it through location and patronage to the most powerful figure within this structure: the patriarch. The scribe designates the patriarch 'commander of the Apostolic Antiochian throne', 'pillar of the Syriac Orthodox Church', and 'promoter of the Syriac Orthodox community'.[128] Importantly, this information also communicates a vision for the manuscript's collective usage and reach. Liturgical texts already had an inherent public dimension as the means by which the lay population – many of whom would have been illiterate – could access the words of scripture.[129] Yet this value is accentuated here by the move to translate the liturgical language of the church – Syriac – into one ostensibly more aligned with the manuscript's 'public' of 'readers and listeners' – Arabic.

---

[125] Murre-van den Berg, *Scribes and Scriptures*, 121–23.

[126] ZFRN 397, p. 679, cc. 1–2. [127] ZFRN 397, p. 683, c. 2.

[128] ZFRN 397, p. 683, c. 2. [129] Krimsti, 'Signatures of Authority', 114.

It could be argued that the 'public' to whom the scribe refers simply indicates the congregation at Saffron Monastery, particularly as he mentions the 'perpetual endowment' of the manuscript to this establishment, which appears to have been honoured. No additional copies of ʿAbd al-Nūr's translated lectionary have been identified either. However, other examples emerging from this context indicate the Syriac Orthodox hierarchy's awareness of changing linguistic customs among their community at large – and their need to respond to this. Between 1739 and 1740, around ten years after MS 397 was copied, Patriarch Shukr Allāh commissioned another Syriac to Arabic translation from ʿAbd al-Nūr. This time, it was ascetic treatises by the Syriac Orthodox scholar Moses bar Kepha (d. 903), preserved in a Syriac Orthodox church in Diyarbakır, a city around eighty kilometres north of Mardin.[130] In the colophon, the scribe records how the patriarch commissioned this translation as the 'Syriac Orthodox community' could no longer 'understand the Syriac language'. According to him, the patriarch perceived that rendering such 'beneficial and righteously orthodox' texts into Arabic could abate 'confusion' and 'heresy' among his flock.[131] Although he does not mention our lectionary, ʿAbd al-Nūr notes that, for the same reason, the patriarch ordered an Arabic translation of another Syriac Orthodox scholar, Jacob of Edessa (d. 708).[132] The impact of these translations, he concludes, would be far-reaching, creating 'a treasure-trove for Christian children and the Syriac Orthodox community'.[133]

The colophons frame these translations as a concerted initiative for linguistic reform and thus religious conformity across the entire Syriac Orthodox community – instituted by the highest authority among them,

---

[130] Diyarbakır, Meryem Ana Kilisesi, MS 3/2. Consulted on the 'HMML Virtual Reading Room, Project No. DIYR 00037', https://w3id.org/vhmml/readingRoom/view/122749 (hereafter DIYR 37).

[131] DIYR 37, ff. 313v–315r.

[132] DIYR 37, f. 314v. I have been unable to locate the autograph, but copies are found in Mardin, Church of the Forty Martyrs, MS 361 (1728–9) and MS 409 (1727–8).

[133] DIYR 37, f. 315r.

Patriarch Shukr Allāh. There are even indications that Syriac was becoming obsolete much further afield. In 1731, a Syriac Orthodox bishop in Damascus, over 500 kilometres from Mardin, noted in a Syriac manuscript that its neglected condition was due to there being 'no readers of Syriac or people who know the language accurately'.[134]

The sense of communal service that MS 397 evokes does not end with its colophon. In fact, a remarkably lengthy collection of beneficial deeds performed by members of the Syriac Orthodox community – mostly patriarchs, but also laypeople – are registered in the final pages of the manuscript. By allowing MS 397 to take on an additional function as a record, these notes arguably reinforce the sense of authority and public significance observed above, and thus merit attention. Having identified his noble patron, the scribe continues:

> and in this very year he [the patriarch] consecrated the chrism in the monastery, and constructed orchard walls outside the monastery. He also went to great lengths to restore damaged objects within the monastery, that is, the altars and sanctuaries.[135]

The act of having the lectionary translated thus joins a range of beneficial acts performed for Saffron Monastery, the core of Syriac Orthodox authority. Strikingly, such use of MS 397 outlived the reign of Shukr Allāh. Overleaf, we encounter the elegant Arabic Karshuni handwriting of Patriarch George IV (1768–81), who served two terms later. In chronological order, the patriarch documents his personal endowments to Saffron Monastery: fifteen silver candelabras in 1751–2 while he was a metropolitan; two silver fans in 1759; two chandeliers, two fans and a silver censer in 1768;

---

[134] Charfet Rahmani, MS 112, f. 245r, consulted in A. Binggeli et al., *Catalogue des manuscrits syriaques et garshuni du Patriarcat syriaque-catholique de Charfet (Liban)* (Darʿun-Harissa: Publications Patriarcales de Charfet, 2021), 421–23.

[135] ZFRN 397, p. 683, c. 2.

renovations to cells and altars in 1772–3; and a large crucifix and chandelier in 1774.[136] A subsequent notice dated 1805–6 by Patriarch Matthew (1782–1819) indicates the manuscript's enduring usage as a record of patriarchal endowments.[137]

The following pages expand the scope of the record by listing donations from the Syriac Orthodox laity. In 1774–5, a certain Sarkīs and Mādah donated grapevines to the monastery; in 1778–9, Wardah and Elia donated a garden; in 1847, Baho ibn ʿAbd Allāh of Banābīl donated an orchard; and in 1909, Istifān and Sawsan Barṣawm of Mosul donated an ecclesiastical vestment.[138] While the authors of these notes are not identified, the orchard donation is witnessed by the signature and seal of Patriarch Jacob II (1847–71).[139] Finally, a scrawled note records the baptism of Yūḥannon ibn Maqdisī Isḥāq at Saffron Monastery in 1936, sealing a documentary legacy which lasted over two hundred years (Figure 5).[140]

From its initial conception to its enduring place of belonging, the MS 397 lectionary has been bound to the centre of Syriac Orthodox authority. Yet, as its numerous paratextual notes indicate, this materialization of patriarchal authority was not envisioned as confined to a clerical elite at Saffron Monastery. Rather, both explicitly and implicitly, it addressed a 'public' defined by a shared religious and linguistic affiliation and a jurisdiction that extended across Upper Mesopotamia. Moreover, it testified to changes occurring within this communal body. It is unlikely that MS 397 itself was widely circulated: as with the documents produced within monastic contexts in thirteenth-century Tibet (discussed in the next section), access to the physical copy may have been restricted even inside the monastery. However, other manuscripts indicate that the disuse of the Syriac language was perceived by Patriarch Shukr Allāh and his contemporaries as a community-wide issue, jeopardizing its stability and cohesion. Though beyond the scope of the present study, MS 397 could even be considered

---

[136] ZFRN 397, p. 684, c. 1; p. 684, c. 2; p. 685, c. 1; p. 685, c. 2; p.686, c. 1.

[137] ZFRN 397, p. 687, c. 1. [138] ZFRN 397, p. 687, c. 1; p. 687, c. 2; p. 688, c. 1.

[139] ZFRN 397, p. 687, c. 2. [140] ZFRN 397, p. 688, c. 1.

Figure 5 Mardin, Dayr Zaʿfarān, MS 397 (HMML Pr. No. ZFRN 00397), p. 687, various endowment notices with subscription and seal of Patriarch Jacob II. Image courtesy of the Dayr Zaʿfarān (Monastery) Mardin, Turkey, and the Hill Museum & Manuscript Library. Published with permission of the owners. All rights reserved.

against broader processes of communal identity development taking place throughout early modern Ottoman society.[141]

Alongside its linguistic agenda, the use of MS 397 to register donations to the patriarchal residence, by prelates and laypeople, implies its continued authoritative and collective connotation. Although Saffron Monastery would become the first location in Mardin to house a printing press in 1881,[142] as the baptism note from 1936 betrays, the esteem for MS 397 outlived this technological advancement.

The 'public' conjured by MS 397 represented a particular segment – and, in its most limited understanding, a particular institution – within the remarkable diversity of early modern Ottoman society. When approaching source materials from such contexts, this diversity requires reflection on *which* public is meant. Not only can the public addressed by a text change over language, location and institution; it can also change depending when and by whom the texts are used.

---

[141] See T. Krstić and D. Terzioğlu, *Entangled Confessionalizations? Dialogic Perspectives on the Politics of Piety and Community Building in the Ottoman Empire, 15th–18th Centuries* (Piscataway: Gorgias Press, 2022).

[142] A. Taşğın and R. Langer, 'The Establishment of the Syrian Orthodox Printing Press', in G. Roper, ed. *Historical Aspects of Printing and Publishing*, 181–92.

Communicating in and beyond the Monastery in Tibet, by Daniel Wojahn

While sometimes the same text and object can communicate to different, expanding circles, at other times different media are used to serve similar purposes. The different tasks and different audiences of the paratext in the manuscript from the 'Saffron Monastery' of Syriac Christians can be contrasted with communication from a monastery in a different tradition, that of thirteenth-century Tibetan Buddhism. Rules and regulations circulated within monasteries, a circumscribed kind of publication; but the same principles were shared with non-literate members of the community, often beyond the monasteries' walls, in spoken word, through proverbs and precepts rather than through written texts. Such a shared 'public', like the groups in the early modern coteries around Edmund Plowden's *Treatise* (see next section) or the linguistic and confessional communities in the Ottoman Empire (see previous section), can be constituted even with spoken discourse.

Writing was already widespread during the time of the first dynasty of the self-proclaimed 'snow country' of Tibet, at least from the seventh century CE. Numerous scribes and editors were employed by the Tibetan administration to produce registers, chronicles and legal documents. A few of these manuscripts survived for over a millennium and to this day paint an intricate picture of a hierarchical society, whose military strength once almost brought the mighty Chinese Tang dynasty (618–906) to its knees.

After the collapse of the Tibetan royal dynasty towards the end of the ninth century, which led to the political fragmentation of the Tibetan plateau, Tibetan culture underwent a profound transformation. Subsequently, as Tibetan authors claimed, Buddhism became a civilizing force in Tibet and social and political discourse was reshaped by the incorporation of Indian Buddhist values and cosmological order. Similarly, legal-administrative documents were subject to a wide range of Buddhist interpretations, from the individual techniques of their arrangement and composition to the ritualized forms of their public presentation.[143]

---

[143] See e.g. F. Pirie, 'Buddhist Law in Early Tibet: The Emergence of an Ideology', *Journal of Law and Religion*, 32 (2017), 406–22.

Yet while monastic institutions played an increasing role in managing public authority and functioned as educational and administrative centres, with abbots exerting considerable influence on local communities, the orality prevalent in Tibetan societies before the advent of Buddhism continued to hold immense importance: proverbs and aphorisms continued to serve as fundamental tools employed by power holders and mediators alike, and most of them are still widely used today.[144]

The institutionalization of Tibetan Buddhism was negotiated on several levels. First, the leading religious figures established important personal relationships with local clan rulers, on whose land the monasteries were built and from where the fields and workers necessary for their maintenance were designated. From the twelfth century, several monasteries experienced an economic boom that was accompanied by an exponential increase in the number of enrolled monks. Furthermore, they became fully fledged enterprises with various revenue streams, one of which was lending money and/or grain to the local population.[145]

With the growing population of monks and the concomitant hiring of more peasants and servants for the upkeep of the monastery, the need for regulations governing community life and sanctions of all kinds also increased. The main guarantor was a multi-tiered system of rules of conduct that required monks and aspirants to take a series of vows. Depending on the monk's or novice's status, the rules to be observed, known as the *Basket of Discipline* (*Vinaya Piṭaka*), increased in scope and complexity and often became the focus of monastic training and study.

---

[144] A good introduction can be found in P. K. Sørensen and F. X. Erhard, 'An Inquiry into the Nature of Tibetan Proverbs', *Proverbium*, 30 (2013), 281–309.

[145] The history of these developments has not yet been sufficiently studied, but see M. Kapstein, *The Tibetan Assimilation of Buddhism: Conversion, Contestation, and Memory* (Oxford: Oxford University Press, 2000); R. Davidson, *Tibetan Renaissance: Tantric Buddhism in the Rebirth of Tibetan Culture* (New York: Columbia University Press, 2005); and P. K. Sørensen and G. Hazod, *Rulers on the Celestial Plain: Ecclesiastic and Secular Hegemony in Medieval Tibet*, 2 vols (Vienna: Österreichischen Akademie der Wissenschaften, 2007).

However, a document from the early thirteenth century testifies that in times of natural disaster or political unrest, it was necessary to issue additional injunctions in the form of open letters reprimanding the misconduct of some community members and giving practical instructions for action. This document *cum* open letter was written by the ageing abbot Jikten Gonpo Rinchen Pel (1143–1217) of the central Tibetan Drigung monastery in response to a severe famine in the 1210s. The abbot appeals to the compassion of the Buddhist community: some monks of the monastery who are involved in money-lending are requested not to force the stricken population to repay loans beyond their means or to prosecute merchants for old debts,[146] which is exemplified beautifully by the Tibetan proverb: 'One thinks of Buddhist teachings when the stomach is full; one thinks of stealing when the stomach is empty.'[147] The document also refers to the existing monastery rules, the validity of which was still declared binding, yet lacked practical instructions in times of crisis. Consequently, the publication of this open letter became necessary.[148] We can assume that the monastic administration circulated or published the letter widely enough to be noted by the at least 2,000 monks living in the monastery at that time.

Jikten Gonpo's close disciple and successor Chennga Drakpa Jungné began his career as abbot at the related Densatil Monastery, some 200 kilometres south of Drigung Monastery, and composed monastery rules for both sees in the 1230s. Chennga Drakpa Jungné had obviously learnt from the experiences of his predecessor and incorporated this passage to Densatil's monastery rules: 'Do not forcibly take the allowances from the

---

[146] Jikten Gonpo Rinchen Pel, 'Gdan Sa Nyams Dmas Su Gyur Skabs Mdzad Pa'i Bca' Yig [Monastery rule produced during the deterioration of the monastic seat]', in *The Collected Works (Bka' 'bum) of Kham Gsum Chos Kyi Rgyal Po Thub Dbang Ratna Śrī (Skyob-Pa 'Jig-Rten-Gsum-Mgon)*, ed. H. H. Drikung Kyabgon Chetsang Konchog Tenzin Kunzang Thinley Lhundub, 12 vols (Delhi: Drikung Kagyu Ratna Shri Sungrab Nyamso Khang, 2001), iv, 126–28.

[147] P. T. Shastri, *Like a Yeti Catching Marmots* (Boston: Wisdom, 2012), 51.

[148] For another open letter in English translation, see D. Wojahn, 'Lama Dampa's Open Letter Promoting Vegetarianism', *Yeshe*, 3 (2023), https://yeshe.org/lama-dampas-open-letter-promoting-vegetarianism/.

monastic subject communities and lay disciples.'[149] Furthermore, both his legal texts shed light on why conveying public authority through such documents was fraught with difficulties. Chennga Drakpa Jungné not only specified who was to implement certain rules, such as the dress code or adherence to a basic curriculum, but he also designated the territorial boundaries of the monastery, thereby delineating the geographical scope of these rules. Moreover, the text demonstrates that the rules were not limited to the religious personnel but also applied to the monastery's subjects living in the area. The colophon then states that this proclamation (*bka' shog*) was to be publicly recited on auspicious occasions.[150]

Although we do not know exactly who attended these public readings, we can nevertheless assume that the rules were 'published' only within the monastery walls and for a limited group. Likewise, only a small elite circle within the monastery had access to the actual documents.[151] To this end, both of Chennga Drakpa Jungné's monastery rules referred to the distinguished conduct of former high dignitaries; the imitation of their actions and lifestyles were prescribed as abstract guidelines for the monks' behaviour, since they did not have access to the documents themselves.

These texts indicate the regulations also applied to workers, guests and travellers. How, then, did these diverse groups learn about them? While it is possible that the local population attended the public proclamations, the vibrant Tibetan oral tradition offers many proverbs and sayings that lent themselves to wide dissemination and conveyed the same messages. In the absence of state law or widely accessible printed legal codes, people employed proverbs – such as 'After one drinks the water of the land, one must abide by the laws of the land'.[152] Although the fixed rules of the

---

[149] Chennga Drakpa Jungné, *The Collected Works (Gsung 'bum) of Grags Pa 'byung Gnas, a Chief Disciple of the Skyob-Pa-'Jig-Rten-Gsum-Mgon, 1175–1255*, ed. H. H. Drikung Kyabgon Chetsang (Delhi: Drikung Kagyu Publications, 2002), 302.

[150] Chennga Drakpa Jungné, *Collected Works*, 306.

[151] B. Jansen, *The Monastery Rules: Buddhist Monastic Organization in Pre-Modern Tibet* (Oakland: University of California Press, 2018), 22.

[152] L. Pemba, *Tibetan Proverbs* (Dharamsala: Library of Tibetan Works and Archives, 1996), 190. Translation is my own.

monastery remained opaque and limited to specific groups, it seems likely that the articulate and versatile idioms and proverbs formed part of a shared knowledge system.

In this context, it seems no coincidence that one of the leading Tibetan scholars known as Sakya Pandita (1182–1251) at about the same time wrote a didactic work entitled *A Precious Treasury of Elegant Sayings*, which popularized Tibetan poetry based on the classical Indian model.[153] Its contents deal with the fundamental concepts, norms and standards of human behaviour and analyze various aspects of people's attitudes and responses to other people and things in their environment, all formulated in easily memorized aphorisms and sayings.

To stay with our example of money lending, we find the following observation in the *Precious Treasury of Elegant Sayings*: 'In this world, there is no certainty that the loans one has made will be repaid.'[154] This echoes one of the precepts from the open letter by Jikten Gonpo, who recommends not lending all of one's possessions, which can only be repaid in old age or after death.[155]

Sakya Pandita is said to have supplemented *A Precious Treasury of Elegant Sayings* with another work entitled *Magical Net of Elegant Sayings*. In it, the author urges his readers to be serious, reliable or broadminded and inspires them to act morally. One such saying is, for example, 'If one is prosperous, one should freeze the interest rate on what is owed'.[156] The aphorism can easily be communicated to merchants and landowners without the intervention of a special written regulation.

---

[153] More on the subject can be found in M. Kapstein, 'The Indian Literary Identity in Tibet', in S. Pollock, ed. *Literary Cultures in History* (Berkeley: University of California Press, 2003), 747–802.

[154] Sakya Pandita, *Legs par bshad pa rin po che'i gter [A Precious Treasury of Elegant Sayings]*, in his *Gsung 'bum (dpe bsdur ma) [Collected Works (critical edition)]*, ed. Dpal brtsegs bod yig dpe rnying zhib 'jug khang, 4 vols. (Beijing: Krung go'i bod rig pa dpe skrun khang, 2007), i, 196–239 (233).

[155] Jikten Gonpo Rinchen Pel, 'Gdan Sa Nyams', 128.

[156] Sakya Pandita, *Legs bshad 'phrul gyi dra ba [Magical Net of Elegant Sayings]*, in his *Gsung 'bum (dpe bsdur ma)*, 529–37 (533).

These examples illustrate how orality permeated more widely than written codes and that the physical object became more of a formality. With Tibetan monastery rules, the manuscript itself was considered precious and edifying. Even if most people were not granted access to the original, most of the rules were well understood by the local population. Although we have no precise information how this knowledge was disseminated in the thirteenth century, we can assume that idiomatic expressions and the like played a significant role in its publication. The actual monastery rules only concerned cases where the rules were regularly broken or were thought to be in need of clarification.

An example of how idiomatic language and proverbs lend themselves to public authority can be found in the political 'Testament' of Jangchup Gyeltsen (1302–64), an influential Tibetan administrator. The text was intended for his successors and describes in minute detail both his political career and the difficulties he experienced along the way. One of his mentors Nyammépa made a point of teaching him parables and phrases that contained lessons about mistakes and misconduct. The teacher told him, 'You should memorise these sayings because it will benefit you and help you to avoid bad behaviour and be free from mistakes. These good sayings are not of the kind that the edicts (of prominent secular or religious rulers) could parcel out.'[157] This anecdote showcases an exceptional application of the concept of edicts, employed here for rhetorical effect. By comparing proverbs to edicts, Nyammépa underscores the unique potency and universality of these folkloric expressions. Unlike the pronouncements – in this case made by the Mongol Qubilai Khan – which are often specific and potentially ephemeral, proverbs and idioms transcend temporal and geographic boundaries, offering timeless wisdom applicable to individuals of all backgrounds and positions, including those wielding public authority.

In thirteenth-century central Tibet, open letters and monastery rules served as authoritative proclamations issued by religious leaders to communicate their policies and principles, and played a central role in negotiating public authority

---

[157] Jangchup Gyeltsen, *Rlangs Kyi Po Ti Bse Ru Rgyas Pa* [*"The Rhinoceros Book"; Biography of the Divine Rlang Lineage*], ed. Tséten Phüntsok (Lhasa: Bod ljong mi dmangs dpe skrun khang, 1986), 133.

and establishing legitimacy. However, these documents were not printed or reproduced but were kept as prized items by the leading monks and authorities – an accrual of aura not unlike that held by some of the manuscripts of great authors kept as literary relics in twentieth-century universities (like those of Samuel Beckett, discussed shortly). Moreover, in addition to the written word, other forms of communication existed in Tibet in the thirteenth and fourteenth centuries, drawing on parables, proverbs and idioms to support the dissemination of exclusive decrees and legal texts. In such utterances, as in genres such as carols (see Chapter 2) or sermons, there is something like a 'public' circulating shared texts, without any physical publication.

Reading Publics and the Elizabethan Succession, by Daniel Haywood

As well as addressing smaller 'publics', each of the examples – in the Syriac church and Tibetan monastery – also reveal one key problem in identifying the 'public' for unprinted media (and probably for printed media too): that the reach of a work can change over time. Unprinted media might, for technological reasons, address smaller publics, but they do not necessarily address single, simple or stable ones. This is a frequent feature of publication beyond the press, but – as always – the exact form it takes varies according to particular political, literary and other contexts. Some of those changing readerships can even become fairly widespread, but not in an immediate or an unchanging way. A good example of this are works that, though composed after the introduction of printing in western Europe, continued to circulate in manuscript. While these manuscript tracts were often produced for a specialist, coterie audience, the reading 'publics' they ultimately addressed were by no means unsubstantial or static. An instructive example is a treatise on the Elizabethan succession by the eminent common lawyer, Edmund Plowden (*c.* 1518–85). Plowden's work shows how a manuscript document produced at the behest of a specific reading 'public' for a specific polemic purpose was later adopted and repurposed through a wider network of readers and kept alive by changing political circumstances.

Plowden's *Treatise of Succession* was written during the Christmas vacation of the Inns of Court 1566–7 in support of Mary, Queen of Scots' claim to the English throne. Plowden set out to prove that Mary's foreign birth did not invalidate her hereditary title, as Protestant polemicists had alleged in print and manuscript.[158] Over the course of his 52,000-word *Treatise*, Plowden advanced a series of innovative legal, historical and constitutional arguments to refute these polemicists, and asserted that their efforts to forestall the Stewart succession were based on an audacious

---

[158] Plowden's *Treatise* refuted a widely circulating manuscript tract by the militant Protestant MP, John Hales, as well as an anonymous printed polemic, *Allegations against the surmisid title of the Qvine of Scotts and the fauorers of the same* (1565).

and ignorant misinterpretation of the common law. Despite never appearing in print, Plowden's *Treatise* exerted a significant influence over the exigent legal and political debates of the late sixteenth and early seventeenth centuries in England and Scotland.[159] To explain how and why Plowden's manuscript tract attracted a series of influential coterie audiences in the half-century after it was written, we must first attend to its inception.

Plowden's *Treatise* was commissioned by Thomas Howard, the fourth duke of Norfolk, almost certainly representing Elizabeth I. While Elizabeth had long hesitated to acknowledge the Queen of Scots' right to succeed her, the birth of Mary's son, Prince James, in June 1566 offered an opportunity for a rapprochement between the two queens. There is a compelling body of evidence to suggest that by January 1567 Elizabeth was close to acknowledging Mary's rights as heir presumptive in England. In December 1566, Elizabeth promised Mary that she would examine the legitimacy of her father's will – which contemporary polemicists had upheld as a barrier against a Scottish succession. Elizabeth also put a case before her judges that enquired whether Henry VIII's statutory legislation made any action prejudicial to his limitation of the succession, such as recognizing Mary as heir apparent to the English throne, a treasonous offence. Plowden's *Treatise* can thus be read as a product of a crown-authorized investigation into the law of the succession, designed to justify a prospective dynastic settlement in favour of the Queen of Scots. Texts produced for a specialist group might nonetheless be imagined or intended for wider dissemination (as in the texts of the 'Saffron Monastery'). Although Plowden's tract was written privately for a small but influential coterie audience, his arguments were clearly intended to persuade a wider reading public – the Protestant political nation – of the legality of the Stewart succession.

However, on the night of 10 February 1567, Mary's husband, Henry, Lord Darnley, was murdered. The fall-out of this infamous historical whodunit fundamentally transformed the English succession crisis and the

---

[159] Plowden's *Treatise* is extant in six manuscripts: London, British Library, Cotton MS Caligula B. iv, and Harley MS 849; Oxford, Bodleian Library, MS Rawlinson A. 124, and MS Don. c. 43; New York, Morgan Library, MS MA 281; New Haven, Lillian Goldman Law Library, MS G. P72.1.

trajectory of Plowden's *Treatise*. The suspicion of Mary's involvement in the murder, possibly in collusion with James Hepburn, the fourth earl of Bothwell (whom she scandalously married in May of the same year), ultimately led to her imprisonment by a cabal of Scottish Lords and her forced abdication in favour of her son, James, in July 1567. Any potential recognition of Mary Stewart as heir presumptive to the English crown was, only a few months after Plowden first began to put together his defence of her title, now impossible. What, then, was to happen to Plowden's *Treatise*?

It seems that the *Treatise* was first presented to Elizabeth and her Privy Council at some point shortly after Darnley's murder, invoking their displeasure. It is almost certainly the case that this discontent was on account of the inopportune delivery of the tract, too late for Elizabeth to make use of its exigent legal arguments, rather than due to the nature of its contents. Importantly, the council's displeasure did not result in any official censure or punishment for Plowden – either of which we might have expected if he had written his *Treatise* unprompted or without official assurances.

With his manuscript tract thus rejected as a dead letter by the audience for whom it was commissioned, we might imagine Plowden to have circumspectly confined the manuscript of his *Treatise* to a drawer in his chamber, while diligently attending to his duties as Treasurer of the Middle Temple or else returning to his task of compiling his manuscript reports on contemporary legal cases into an innovative volume ready for the press. Interestingly, Plowden claimed to have been 'violently inforced' to print his reports in 1571, upon learning that the manuscript copies he had loaned to his colleagues had been purloined and corrupted by unscrupulous clerks and were set to be printed without his permission (similarly to the unauthorized dissemination of Greek and Latin literature discussed in Chapter 1).[160] If we take Plowden at his word here, we might therefore say that his reports were published *before* print, and that their author was well aware of both the positives and the perils of the scribal networks that existed at the Inns of Court.

---

[160] E. Plowden, *Les Comentaries, ou les Reportes* (London: Tottell, 1571), Preface. Asserting an imprimatur for print based on one's manuscripts being stolen and bastardized by unscrupulous scribes was not uncommon in early modern English literature.

Although Darnley's murder may seem like a date after which Plowden's *Treatise* would have ceased to be useful, potentially rendering it obsolete, evidence offered by Plowden's son Francis provides a surprising insight into the afterlife and revivification of the *Treatise*. In the early seventeenth century, he prepared a presentation copy of the *Treatise* for King James VI and I of Scotland and England.[161] In his dedication to the king, Francis describes how his father had revised his *Treatise* in the late 1560s to prepare it for print. Francis suggests that if Elizabeth's Treason Act of 1571 had not forbidden 'all speache of any successor to this ymperiall Crowne', then his father's *Treatise* would have gone to press in the early 1570s.[162] This assertion is remarkable, especially considering that it outright contradicts a disclaimer found in manuscripts of an early recension of the *Treatise*, that Plowden had no 'intent to publishe' his tract but wrote only to satisfy a private audience.[163] While textual variants between the extant manuscript witnesses indicate that substantial revisions were indeed made to the *Treatise* (almost certainly by Edmund Plowden), it is unlikely that they were made with a mind to publication in print. By the early 1570s Mary was a prisoner in England, having fled captivity in Scotland, and had already become a figurehead for conspiracy and threats to Elizabeth's royal author-ity. In this climate, it would have been uncharacteristically reckless for Plowden to have contemplated printing his *Treatise*. Even before the passing of the Treason Act, Plowden could have been expected to be severely punished for going to press without the Queen's approval. It was only the protections offered to Plowden by the Duke of Norfolk, likely operating on behalf of the Queen, that persuaded him to write his *Treatise* in the first instance; even when writing for a private audience, Plowden nonetheless acknowledged the grave danger in dealing with titles of king-doms, especially for a mere subject such as himself.[164]

---

[161] Oxford, Bodleian Library, MS Don. c. 43.

[162] 13 Eliz. I, c. 1. See J. Raithby et al., ed., *The Statutes of the Realm*, 11 vols. (London: Record Commission, 1819), iv, 526–28.

[163] London, British Library, Harley MS 849, f. 1r.

[164] London, British Library, Harley MS 849, f. 1r–v.

However, compelling evidence suggests that during the period of revision indicated by Francis Plowden (i.e. 1567–71), Plowden senior continued to be involved privately in advocating for Mary Stewart's restoration in Scotland and for her succession to the English crown. In October 1571, John Leslie, bishop of Ross, Mary's ambassador to Elizabeth since September 1568, was imprisoned in the Tower of London for his involvement in the Ridolfi plot. Under threat of torture, he indicated that Plowden (among others) had cautiously offered him assistance in the preparation of his own printed tract in defence of the Stewart succession. It is evident from Leslie's *A defence of the honour of the right highe, mightye and noble Princesse Marie Quene of Scotlande* (1569) that he must have had access to a copy of Plowden's *Treatise*. It is, therefore, quite possible that the substantial revisions to Plowden's *Treatise* were made surreptitiously in the late 1560s for ready inclusion into the first printed edition of Leslie's *Defence*. In this admittedly indirect sense, then, Plowden's case for the Stewart succession was eventually published in print. As Leslie's tract was reissued, in different versions, from various English and Continental presses over the next two decades, the legal and historical arguments originally put forward by Plowden provoked a rash of responses. For instance, William Cecil commissioned two substantial manuscript refutations in the 1580s, written by the Somerset herald Robert Glover and the London recorder and common lawyer William Fleetwood, respectively.

We might thus identify a pattern within the literature of the early Elizabethan succession debate. In 1563, John Hales produced an enormously influential manuscript treatise asserting the invalidity of the Stewart succession, on the grounds that a foreign-born person could not inherit the crown. Hales's arguments were subsequently endorsed in the printed polemic, *Allegations Against*, the publication of which in December 1565 incensed both Elizabeth and Mary and ultimately led to Plowden's pro-Stewart response in 1567. Although still unpublished in print, Plowden's legal, historical and constitutional arguments were then popularized by Leslie's *Defence*, first published in 1569. As mentioned, subsequent reprints of Leslie's *Defence* in the 1580s provoked state-sponsored manuscript refutations by Glover and Fleetwood. We can, then, witness continuing and interconnected uses of both print and manuscript for publication. Manuscript was often used as a medium of response, as an effective means of ensuring that the arguments advanced in printed tracts did not unduly prejudice public debate. Plowden, for instance, feared that if the vitriolic anti-Scottish and anti-Catholic arguments of the printed tract, *Allegations Against*, reached the 'unlearned' public without his confutation, the wider reading public would be 'made ignorant by the ignorant'.[165] While manuscript tracts such as Plowden's *Treatise* perhaps did not circulate as widely as their printed counterparts, at least until they themselves were endorsed in print, it is evident that the noblemen, statesmen and lawyers who were particularly invested in the Elizabethan succession were reading and circulating these important tracts in manuscript. Among these specialized reading publics, the succession debate was influenced equally by manuscript and print.

Following Mary Stewart's execution in February 1587, Plowden's manuscript *Treatise* attracted a new, and surprising, readership. Plowden and Leslie's arguments, initially crafted in response to English Protestant attacks on the Catholic Queen of Scots' claim, were revivified by the Protestant supporters of her son's claim to the English throne, after his hereditary title had been seriously challenged by the Jesuit Robert Persons. Even after James was eventually seated on the English throne from March 1603, manuscript copies of Plowden's tract continued to circulate. Indeed, of the six extant manuscript witnesses of Plowden's *Treatise*, four have been approximately dated to the early to mid-1600s. Seventeenth-century interest in the *Treatise* was likely driven by the debates about the union of the English and Scottish crowns that followed James I's accession. Debates over the naturalization of James's Scottish subjects in England, for instance, brought new relevance to Plowden's constitutional discussion of the respective common law rights of Englishmen and aliens. One of the most prominent supporters of James's union proposals, Sir Robert Cotton, tellingly loaned his manuscript copy of Plowden's *Treatise* to members of the Privy Council not long after James's accession.[166] The arguments of Francis

---

[165] London, British Library, Harley MS 849, f. 1r.

[166] C. G. C. Tite, *The Early Records of Robert Cotton's Library: Formation, Cataloguing, Use* (London: British Library, 2003), 73–74.

Bacon, Sir Edward Coke and the other lawyers involved in *Calvin's Case* (1608) would have also stimulated fresh interest in the first five chapters of Plowden's *Treatise*, which systematically describe the king's two bodies.

As late as the 1670s, the renowned jurist, Sir Matthew Hale – whose copy of the *Treatise* still survives – was citing 'Mr. *Plowden's* learned tract touching the right of succession of *Mary* queen of *Scotland*', as a useful resource for lawyers and political theorists interested in the principles of the succession of the crown.[167] (Hale's treatise was first written circa 1670 but was only printed posthumously owing to his refusal to publish his works during his lifetime.) Reading Hale's treatise on criminal law two centuries later still, the lawyer Ralph Thomas mistakenly assumed that Plowden's *Treatise* had likely been published in print for Hale to have thus encouraged his contemporaries to consult it.[168] However, that Hale cited Plowden's arguments as expedient (and accessible) in the mid-seventeenth century, despite the *Treatise* never appearing in print, is testament to the relative ability of the 'learned tract' to reach a wider reading 'public' even without print.

Likely commissioned by Elizabeth, who perhaps intended to make a version of Plowden's arguments publicly available, if she recognized the Queen of Scots as heir presumptive to the English throne, Plowden's *Treatise* might have become obsolete when shifting political circumstances made such a recognition impossible. Yet by circulating a revised version of his work in manuscript among the coterie of lawyers and political actors who surrounded Mary's arch-defender, John Leslie, Plowden did eventually see his arguments popularized in print via Leslie's *Defence*. Meanwhile, Plowden's *Treatise* continued to be circulated, consulted and copied in manuscript later still: its arguments kept alive by the legal and constitutional crises of the late-Elizabethan succession and the union debates of the early Stuart period. Although originally prepared for one specific coterie, then, Plowden's manuscript *Treatise* found new reading

[167] M. Hale, *Historia Placitorum Coronae: The History of the Pleas of the Crown*, 2 vols (London: Nutt and Gosling, 1736), i, 324.

[168] R. Thomas, 'Edmund Plowden', *Notes and Queries*, 270 (1867), 184.

publics over time, who seized on different aspects of the work in response to need and circumstance.

The question is not whether this is publishing – it is definitely 'going public' to some degree, and the intention and ability to address a wider readership were evident from the outset of Plowden's work. The question is rather to which public and how large a public this publication is addressed, and how it changed over time. While Plowden's experience of being "inforced' to print his legal reports in 1571' reveals that he saw risks in manuscript circulation, just as there were in print, manuscript circulation gave him the opportunity to address a public of a different size and nature. And its continuing circulation allowed the work itself to address a different public over time, and long after Plowden's death.

Samuel Beckett and 'The Life of the Afterlife', by Brian M. Moore

For some authors, a concern for the reception of their unprinted works extends beyond the boundaries of their lives. From Vergil to Geoffrey Chaucer, classical and medieval authors worried about or imagined their works escaping their control. Matthew Hale, for instance, refused to allow the publication of his work during his lifetime (as was just noted). Yet attempts to manage reception (posthumous or otherwise) are always snagged by the complex and compromised agencies inherent in publishing (which we explored earlier) and the tendency for reading publics to mutate in ways unforeseen by the author. Johann Wolfgang von Goethe (1749–1832) fretted over depriving 'posterity' of his unpublished papers: aged seventy-nine, conspicuously absent from a gathering at his own home, Goethe was interrupted in his study by Jenny von Gustedt, who found him perusing some scattered papers. When von Gustedt reminded Goethe of his guests downstairs, he fired back:

> So what [*Ach was*], . . . do you think, little girl, that I will rush to anyone who waits for me? What would become of all this? . . . When I'm dead, nobody will bother [with his old papers]. Tell them that. . . . An old man who still wishes to work cannot suit everyone; if he does, posterity would be displeased.[169]

Two centuries of German textual scholarship has shown that 'posterity' did 'bother' with his papers. Indeed, it has been remarked that the 'ideology of "genius"' prevailing in eighteenth-century Europe induced a deeper concern with the preservation of manuscripts; the copious archives spawned by the German *Sturm und Drang* movement (of which Goethe was a significant proponent) testify to this phenomenon.[170] By the twentieth century, authors agonizing over the futurity of their unpublished work had become a biographical commonplace – there is, perhaps, no greater example of

---

[169] L. Braun, *Im Schatten der Titanen: Erinnerungen an Baronin Jenny von Gustedt* (Berlin: Knaur, 1929), 100. My translation.

[170] D. Van Hulle, 'Modern Manuscripts', in *Oxford Research Encyclopaedia of Literature* (Oxford University Press, 2019).

this than Franz Kafka's 'last request' for his manuscripts to be 'burned unread'.[171] One modern author who took great pains over the fates of his unpublished and published texts beyond the grave and whose manuscripts have had an unexpected 'life of the afterlife' in other media is Samuel Beckett (1906–89).[172] This Irish novelist, playwright and poet, who was resident in France for most of his life, is well-known for plays such as *Waiting for Godot* and *Endgame* and his post-war 'trilogy' of novels (*Molloy*, *Malone Dies* and *The Unnamable*). Across his life, Beckett accumulated a personal archive of unpublished materials ranging from notes on his philosophical reading to complete yet jettisoned texts. Though he passed many of these on to institutional archives during his life, his death prompted the publication of many texts. For instance, despite his hostility to any kind of funeral, he inscribed his final work, 'Comment dire' (self-translated as 'what is the word'), with the injunction 'Keep! for end', almost indicating that he wished for his final 'word' to be uttered post-mortem.[173]

Beckett's prickly coquettishness regarding publication was inherited early on, supposedly from his mentor of sorts, James Joyce, who was similarly plagued by publication difficulties, albeit for different reasons. (Joyce's *Dubliners*, virtually complete by 1905, went unpublished until 1914 due to publishers' fears about possible obscenity; *Ulysses* prompted an obscenity trial.) Beckett's well-known recalcitrance towards theatrical interpretations of his plays mirrors his eagle eye for misprints or, worse still, editorial changes to his printed works. *Murphy* (1938), Beckett's first published novel, was rejected no fewer than forty times – in part, due to his reluctance to accept his publisher's requests for cuts and emendations. *Murphy*, however, had precedents: Beckett's first attempt at a novel, *Dream of Fair to Middling Women* (1932), was roundly rejected by publishers (and would only be published, in accordance with Beckett's wishes, a year after his death); a subsequent collection of short stories, *More Pricks*

---

[171] Quoted in M. Brod, 'Postscripts', in Franz Kafka, *The Trial*, trans. W. Muir and E. Muir (New York: Modern Library, 1956), 326–38 (328).

[172] S. Beckett, *Mercier and Camier*, ed. S. Kennedy (London: Faber, 2011), 101.

[173] Reading, University of Reading Library, MS UoR-3316 ['*Comment dire/what is the word* notebook'], f. 2r.

than Kicks (1934), was nearly consigned to the same fate, for similar reasons of obscurity and 'Joyceanism'. The texts that brought Beckett fame, the post-war 'trilogy' of novels and *En attendant Godot*, were accepted by Éditions de Minuit at a time when Beckett despaired of ever seeing them in print. Due to his notorious shyness in this period, it was his partner, Suzanne Deschevaux-Dumesnil, who entered publishing houses and spoke to editors while Beckett anxiously waited across the road.

Things changed in 1969, when Beckett received the Nobel Prize for Literature. His French, English and German publishers wished to capitalize on this publicity by publishing some earlier 'rejected' works. Jérôme Lindon, Minuit's editor, was determined to publish *Mercier et Camier* (written, and abandoned, in 1946). Previously, Beckett had envisaged its publication alongside other scrapped works in a collection entitled 'Merdes Posthumes', perhaps an ancestor of 'Keep! for end'.[174] Though Beckett was a scrupulous curator of what could and could not be published, as well as when, where and in which language, as a Nobel Laureate he found that his time was increasingly spent on drip-feeding his archive to the public. Following his death, this role has changed hands, becoming the purview of scholars, digital archivists and publishers – each introducing their own curatorial hang-ups.

Though Beckett has long been recognized as an uneasy bedfellow of literary 'modernism' – the early twentieth-century movement whose best-known practitioners in the English language include Joyce, T.S. Eliot and Virginia Woolf – [175] his attitude to publication was quintessentially modernist. In tracing modernism's antagonistic negotiations between cultural elitism and mass media, Lawrence Rainey argues that, through publishing

---

[174] Beckett, quoted in S. Weller, 'Beckett's Last Chance: Les Éditions de Minuit', in M. Nixon, ed. *Publishing Samuel Beckett* (London: British Library, 2011), 113–30 (123).

[175] Anthony Cronin, *Samuel Beckett: The Last Modernist* (London: Flamingo, 1997), dubbed Beckett the 'last modernist'; Fredric Jameson, *Postmodernism or, The Cultural Logic of Late Capitalism* (London: Verso, 1989), and Tyrus Miller, *Late Modernism: Politics, Fiction, and the Arts Between the World Wars* (Berkeley: University of California Press, 1999), describe Beckett as a 'late modernist'.

and marketing practices, the early-twentieth-century avant-garde chiselled out its place in the cultural sphere by resurrecting a literary 'aristocracy' within 'the world of the commodity'.[176] While modernist art acquiesces to commodification, it does so on its own terms: rejecting the 'ephemerality' and mass-production of popular media, modernist art was marketed as a savvy investment – the cultural (as well as commercial) value of modernism promised to accrue. Scholars have shown that this practice was on display during literary modernism's hallowed *annus mirabilis*, 1922: the year of Joyce's *Ulysses*, Eliot's *The Waste Land*, Woolf's *Jacob's Room* and Marcel Proust's death.[177] One iconoclastic study of the 'Beckett Industry' argues, perhaps over-cynically, that Beckett and his acolytes, through myriad strategies (including 'publicity shots') consciously established a 'Beckett "brand"': just as modernism sought to revalue its commodification through the rubric of investment, Beckett sought celebrity through self-advertised reclusiveness.[178] As such, this Beckett becomes 'a commodified postmodern anti-commodity, more Innocent smoothie than Coca Cola'.[179] To some degree, Beckett's late texts capitalize on this awkward relationship with literary value.[180] The conclusory paragraph of *Ill Seen Ill Said* (1981) garishly reproduces the notion of textual 'consumption': the narrative voice, it seems, grows jaws and swallows the remaining 'crumb[s] of carrion' that comprise Beckett's paltry world. Before the novella's final, dubious dictum – 'Know happiness' – its dénouement figures narrative culmination in digestive terms: 'Lick chops and basta'.[181] The paradox of Beckett's late works is that despite their density and brevity – and their

[176] L. Rainey, *Institutions of Modernism: Literary Elites and Public Culture* (New Haven: Yale University Press, 1998), 39.

[177] See M. North, *Reading 1922: A Return to the Scene of the Modern* (Oxford: Oxford University Press, 1999).

[178] S. J. Dilks, *Samuel Beckett in the Literary Marketplace* (New York: Syracuse University Press, 2011).

[179] P. D. McDonald, 'Calder's Beckett', in M. Nixon, ed. *Publishing*, 153–70 (155).

[180] S. Connor, *Theory and Cultural Value* (Oxford: Blackwell, 1992), 80–9.

[181] S. Beckett, *Company/Ill Seen Ill Said/Worstward Ho/Stirrings Still*, ed. D. Van Hulle (London: Faber, 2009), 78.

internal repudiation of 'value' – they are caught in the matrix of literary value: their resistance to commodification is part and parcel of why they are so eminently desirable. In monetary terms, one might bristle at the £1000 price-tag affixed to a deluxe edition of Beckett's last-published text, *Stirrings Still* (1988) – equating to £40 per page. (Copies today typically go for much more.) For an author thematically obsessed with austerity, Beckett's published works often connoted luxury. While this tendency has been acknowledged regarding published works, his manuscripts also acquired comparable commodity value. Although the sociology of Beckett's printed texts has a firm bedrock in scholarship, the sociology of *unprinted* texts has been more slippery.

Like any modernist worth their salt, Beckett knew the value of his manuscripts. He sold them, though, early on, for unknowingly meagre amounts; he gave them as gifts to friends and fellow artists; he allowed their exhibition in university libraries; he exchanged them for paintings (suggesting a recognition of their status as art objects); he encouraged the publication of variorum editions of drafts (and in 1986, he wrote that it was 'high time' that such a project began);[182] in his will Beckett bequeathed the remainder to various institutions. There is an obvious distinction between Beckett's selling, gifting and bartering of his manuscripts and his donation of papers to another 'institution of modernism', university archives. In 1971, James Knowlson, a lecturer at the University of Reading, telephoned Beckett to request some material for an exhibition on his work. Over the next two decades, Beckett regularly sent a shopping bag or small suitcase crammed with manuscripts, annotated books and other papers to Reading's growing archive. 1971 is a watershed moment for the curation of Beckett's unpublished works (now dubbed his 'grey canon').[183] That the majority of Beckett's papers are currently retained in a few key archives (Reading University, the Harry Ransom Centre, Trinity College Dublin and the

---

[182] Beckett, quoted in D. Van Hulle, 'The Text as Figure and Ground: Beckett and Electronic Publishing', in M. Nixon, ed. *Publishing*, 219–28 (219).

[183] S. E. Gontarski, 'Greying the Canon: Beckett and Performance', in S. E. Gontarski and A. Uhlmann, eds. *Beckett after Beckett* (Gainesville: University Press of Florida, 2006), 141–57.

Bibliothèque nationale de France) testifies to his adoption of a more careful attitude towards the posterity of his scribblings. Knowlson would regularly receive a small suitcase or a shopping bag from the Galeries Lafayette crammed with manuscripts, annotated books and other papers for the growing archive at Reading. The later Beckett was, in a sense, writing for two audiences: the contemporary reader and the future archival researcher, the second no doubt breathing down his neck as he crossed out 'give-away' references to his childhood in Dublin and added quotations from Dante's *Commedia* in the margins of his ever-denser works.

In Beckett's case, the line between published and unpublished works is often blurred. From the 1960s onwards, Beckett counterintuitively publishes 'drafts' (typically in magazines) and abandons fleshed-out projects capriciously. His excessively self-denigrating language about the work of this period frames each new text as a waste product of a previous failure: his writing is a 'work in regress' or '6 mois de ratures', his texts are 'abortions', 'gasps', 'shit' and 'wreckage', and – instead of concluding a work – he discards them or passes on draft material to his publishers.[184] Titles such as 'Faux Départs', 'From an Abandoned Work', 'From an Unabandoned Work', *Residua* and *Disjecta* suggest a growing interest in the finished-unfinished, or the work-across-works in Beckett's publishing practices. From this perspective, Beckett's archive resembles a warren from which published texts, almost accidentally, poke out their heads.

Oddly, in the decades since his death, this phenomenon has become more prevalent. As Peter Fifield notes, due to the constant 'drip-feed' of archival material into the public sphere, Beckett has become 'newly prolific' beyond the grave: 'Beckett is more alive now than he has been since he was *actually* alive.'[185] This is in no small part due to the foundation of the Beckett Digital Manuscripts Project (BDMP), which has published digital editions of Beckett's manuscripts and provided a partial digitization of his library. Alongside images of the original documents, the online archive

---

[184] Beckett, Samuel, *Letters*, ed. G. Craig, 4 vols. (Cambridge: Cambridge University Press, 2009), iii, 619, 622, 628; iv, 35.

[185] P. Fifield, 'Samuel Beckett: Out of the Archive, An Introduction', *Modernism/Modernity*, 18 (2011), 675.

provides searchable transcriptions, hyperlinks between manuscripts and reading traces in the library (often illustrating cryptic allusions), and a means of comparing variants across drafts. The democratic reach of the digital archive (available through a library subscription) further complicates the way in which we consider Beckett's 'value': manuscripts that were previously sold to private collectors are now steadily distributed to the public (excepting those few which remain in private hands). Not only is Beckett more alive and prolific than ever, but his writing also appears less alien and potentially (to use an un-Beckettian term) more 'knowable'.

A sense of nostalgia for the highpoint of literary modernism has been reflected by the publication of reams of draft materials from the period in the past half-century. Commenting on this trend, Hannah Sullivan notes that the transmission of such material from the archive to the public sphere necessitates a 'Fall' from the lively possibilities of the archive into the editorial 'postlapsarian world of fixity'.[186] This is an image that no doubt would have appealed to Beckett's morbid, quasi-theological sensibilities. However, as often with Beckett, the reduction of the dying to the dead, of the falling to the fallen, is easier said than done. To accommodate this peculiarity, Dirk Van Hulle describes the BDMP as a 'continuum' that will one day digitally incorporate the entirety of Beckett's literary 'travail', both published and unpublished within his lifetime.[187] Instead of a stable chronology of publication dates indicating a succession of completed works, a messier continuum of writing is the BDMP's intention. As Beckett's œuvre, beyond the grave, stretches its boundaries, there is a sense that the BDMP is continuously deferring its fall into fixity; yet, even if such an ideal 'Complete Writings' were realisable, I suspect that the 'Complete Beckett', obsessed as he was with absences and silences, might still slip through those nets.

---

[186] H. Sullivan, 'Why Do Authors Produce Textual Variation on Purpose? Or, Why Publish a Text That Is Still Unfolding?', *Variants*, 12–13 (2016), 77–103 (98).

[187] D. Van Hulle, 'Introduction: A Beckett Continuum', in D. Van Hulle, ed., *The New Cambridge Companion to Samuel Beckett* (Cambridge: Cambridge University Press, 2015), xvii–xxvi (xxv).

4 Conclusion

Fixity is something that we have queried as one of the endpoints of publication in various of our examples: liturgical books, the wording of carols and plays as performed or as printed could all vary, and publication – dissemination to others – does not pin down the text but propagates its variation. In tandem, we have questioned the idea of publishing as a one-off process or moment: like Daniel W. Hobbins, who suggested that works published by medieval ecclesiastics could advance through a continuing set of 'publishing moments',[188] we have registered processes of publication that could change over time, say, in shifting between different coteries over generations or in moves from authorial papers to digital archives after an author's death. Such posthumous editions test the limits of the term *publication*, which often seems to imply some degree of agency by the creator in a way that *transmission* does not.[189] Yet we have also – another of Hobbins's points – [190] noted multiple agents behind such publishing moments, beyond a single author: stone-carvers or actors who transmit words wholly or partly of another's devising; scribes who rework others' words in passing; monastic communities whose internal and highly specialized rules seeped into a shared and public knowledge system via the vernacular and widespread proverbs; journalists who rely on AI to contribute to their text. And we have noted the different extents of audiences for such publications. Some address a large public, such as the ancient Athenian *polis*, the *literati* of the ancient Roman elite, the theatre-goers of the early modern city – all of which could be considered a 'public' for publishing. Others address smaller communities, such as the members of religious institutions, in traditions across multiple faiths and nations, or small groups with shared political views or even just the family gazing on their daughter's gravestone. But some degree of circulation beyond one private addressee pertains in all our cases. Works were shared with audiences over all manner of scales and time-scales, with all manner of agents and recipients, in all manner of media. The process is one of communication

---

[188] Hobbins, *Authorship*, 155.   [189] Tahkokallio, *Anglo-Norman*, 9.
[190] Hobbins, *Authorship*, 155.

to others, and if we call this publication, that decentres the modern printed publishing industry – just as is happening in the contemporary media landscape.

Reflecting on these other modes of communication has given us the tools to rethink what publishing is, as what we used to think publishing was deforms, transforms and reforms into multiple new configurations. Yet if we and others upset the term *publication* so much, then does it cease to be a useful term? We find ourselves – if we exchange the word *publication* for the more modest *pot* – in a similar bind to Watt, the protagonist of Samuel Beckett's novel *Watt*, whose semantic zeal results in an inability to call a pot a 'pot':

> Looking at a pot, for example, or thinking of a pot, at one of Mr Knott's pots, of one of Mr Knott's pots, it was in vain that Watt said, Pot, pot. . . . For it was not a pot, the more he looked, the more he reflected, the more he felt sure of that, that it was not a pot at all. It resembled a pot, it was almost a pot, but it was not a pot of which one could say, Pot, pot, and be comforted.

Watt concludes that he would prefer 'on the whole' to deal with 'things of which he did not know the name' than 'things of which the known name, the proven name, was not the name any more for him'; like pots, acts of publication differ from instance to instance and some, like Mr Knott's pots, now resist their 'known name'.[191] While the term *publication* might seem anachronistic if tied to the medium of print, we echo Harold Love in arguing that '*there is no problem about recovering it*' for other media in many cultures and eras.[192] It is useful, in the way that Jaakko Tahkokallio suggested (quoted at the start of Chapter 1) to understand *publication* as a 'metaphorical concept' – no more anachronistic than the names of many nations or 'periods' we study – that allows us to group for comparison many diverse phenomena of 'the joint *releasing* and *disseminating* of content'.[193]

[191] S. Beckett, *Watt*, ed. C. J. Ackerley (London: Faber, 2009) p. 67.
[192] Love, *Scribal Publication*, 35. [193] Tahkokallio, 'Theories', 377.

This allows us to recognize activities which many cultures and people share in, while simultaneously identifying what is special about each particular case. As a heuristic, identifying publication beyond the press is a useful manoeuvre: it lets us argue for the interest of, and to understand better, unprinted media of all kinds, and to ask rather than assert what might count as publication. Now, more than at any point in the last five centuries of the 'Gutenberg Parenthesis', this is a vital intellectual undertaking.

Bibliography

Unprinted Sources

Aberystwyth, National Library of Wales, Brogyntyn MS ii.1.

Berlin, Preußischer Kulturbesitz, P.Berol. inv. 9875.

Cambridge, Trinity College, MS O.3.58.

Cambridge, University Library, MS Ee.1.12.

Charfet Rahmani, MS 11.

Diyarbakır, Meryem Ana Kilisesi, MS 3/2.

Heidelberg, University Library, MS cpg 67.

London, British Library, inv.131v.

London, British Library, Additional MS 5665.

London, British Library, Additional MS 31042.

London, British Library, Cotton MS Caligula B. iv.

London, British Library, Harley MS 849.

Mardin, Church of the Forty Martyrs, MS 40.

Mardin, Church of the Forty Martyrs, MS 361.

Mardin, Dayr Zaʿfarān, MS 397.

New Haven, Lillian Goldman Law Library, MS G. P72.1.

New York, Morgan Library, MS MA 281.

Oxford, Balliol College, MS 354.

Oxford, Bodleian Library, MS Arch. Selden B. 26.

Oxford, Bodleian Library, MS Don. c. 43.

Oxford, Bodleian Library, MS Eng. poet e.1.

Oxford, Bodleian Library, MS Rawlinson A. 124.

Oxford, Lincoln College, MS Lat. 141.

Reading, University of Reading Library, MS UoR-3316.

Printed Works Cited

A New Miscellany for the Year 1737 (London: Osborn, 1737).

Anderson, B., *Imagined Communities: Reflections on the Origins and Spread of Nationalism*, rev. ed. (London: Verso, 1991).

Aulus Gellius, *Attic Nights*, ed. J. C. Rolfe, 3 vols. (Cambridge, MA: Harvard University Press, 1946–52).

Ayalon, A., *The Arabic Print Revolution: Cultural Production and Mass Readership* (Cambridge: Cambridge University Press, 2016).

Backler, K., 'Sisterhood, Affection and Enslavement in Hyperides' *Against Timandrus*', *Classical Quarterly*, 72(2) (2022), 469–86.

Baron, N. S., *Words Onscreen* (Oxford: Oxford University Press, 2015).

Beckett, S., *Company/Ill Seen Ill Said/Worstward Ho/Stirrings Still*, ed. D. Van Hulle (London: Faber, 2009).

Watt, ed. C. J. Ackerley (London: Faber, 2009).

Letters, ed. G. Craig, 4 vols. (Cambridge: Cambridge University Press, 2009).

Mercier and Camier, ed. S. Kennedy (London: Faber, 2011).

Berger, A. M. B., *Medieval Music and the Art of Memory* (Los Angeles: University of California Press, 2005).

Berti, I., 'Quanto costa incidere una stele? Costi di produzione e meccanismi di pubblicazione delle iscrizioni pubbliche in Grecia', *HISTORIKA: Studi di storia greca e romana*, 3 (2014), 11–46.

Bevis, R. W., *The Laughing Tradition: Stage Comedy in Garrick's Day* (Athens: University of Georgia Press, 1980).

Binder, G., 'Öffentliche Autorenlesungen. Zur Kommunikation zwischen Römischen Autoren und ihrem Publikum', in G. Binder and K. Ehlich, eds., *Kommunikation durch Zeichen und Wort* (Trier: Wissenschaftlicher Verlag, 1995), 265–332.

Binggeli, A., Briquel-Chatonnet, F., Debié, M., et al., *Catalogue des manuscrits syriaques et garshuni du Patriarcat syriaque-catholique de Charfet (Liban)* (Dar'un-Harissa: Publications Patriarcales de Charfet, 2021).

Bourgain, P., 'La naissance officielle de l'œuvre: l'expression métaphorique de la mise au jour', in O. Weijers, ed., *Vocabulaire du livre et de l'écriture au Moyen Age* (Turnhout: Brepols, 1989), 195–205.

Braun, L., *Im Schatten der Titanen: Erinnerungen an Baronin Jenny von Gustedt* (Berlin: Knaur, 1929).

Brod, M., 'Postscripts', in F. Kafka, *The Trial*, trans. W. Muir and E. Muir (New York: Modern Library, 1956), 326–38.

Brooke, H., *Gustavus Vasa, the Deliverer of His Country: A Tragedy – As It Was to Have Been Acted at the Theatre-Royal in Drury-Lane* (London: Dodsley, 1739).

Burzachechi, M., 'Oggetti parlanti nelle epigrafi greche', *Epigraphica: Rivista italiana di epigrafia*, 24 (1962), 5–34.

Cave, S., 'The Problem with Intelligence: Its Value-Laden History and the Future of AI', *Proceedings of the AAAI/ACM Conference on AI, Ethics, and Society* (New York: ACM, 2020), 29–35.

Chambers, R. W., and Daunt, M., eds., *A Book of London English, 1384–1425* (Oxford: Clarendon Press, 1931).

Chennga Drakpa Jungné, *The Collected Works (Gsung 'bum) of Grags pa 'byung gnas, 1175–1255*, ed. H. H. Drikung Kyabgön Chetsang (Delhi: Drikung Kagyu Publications, 2002).

Connor, S., *Theory and Cultural Value* (Oxford: Blackwell, 1992).

Cronin, A., *Samuel Beckett: The Last Modernist* (London: Flamingo, 1997).

Davidson, R., *Tibetan Renaissance: Tantric Buddhism in the Rebirth of Tibetan Culture* (New York: Columbia University Press, 2005).

Davies, J. K., 'Accounts and Accountability in Classical Athens', in R. Osborne and S. Hornblower, eds., *Ritual, Finance, Politics: Athenian Democratic Accounts* (Oxford: Clarendon Press, 1994), 201–12.

Del Corso, L., *Il libro nel mondo antico: Archeologia e storia (secoli VII a.C.-IV d.C.)* (Roma: Carocci, 2022).

Dilks, S. J., *Samuel Beckett in the Literary Marketplace* (New York: Syracuse University Press, 2011).

Diodorus Siculus, *Library of History*, ed. C. H. Oldfather, C. L. Sherman, F. R. Walton et al., 12 vols. (Cambridge, MA: Harvard University Press, 1963–71).

Dortmund, A., *Römisches Buchwesen um die Zeitenwende: War T. Pomponius Atticus (110–32 v. Chr.) Verleger?* (Wiesbaden: Harrassowitz, 2001).

El Shamsy, A., *Rediscovering the Islamic Classics: How Editors and Print Culture Transformed an Intellectual Tradition* (Princeton: Princeton University Press, 2020).

Erginbaş, V., 'Enlightenment in the Ottoman Context: Ibrahim Mütefferika and His Intellectual Landscape', in G. Roper, ed., *Historical Aspects of Printing and Publishing in Languages of the Middle East* (Leiden: Brill, 2013), 53–100.

Esposito, E., *Artificial Communication: How Algorithms Produce Social Intelligence* (Cambridge, MA: MIT Press, 2022).

Evans, S. K., Pearce, K. E., Vitak, J., and Treem, J. W., 'Explicating Affordances: A Conceptual Framework for Understanding Affordances in Communication Research', *Journal of Computer-Mediated Communication*, 22 (2017), 35–52.

Feodorov, I., *Arabic Printing for the Christians in Ottoman Lands: The East-European Connection* (Berlin: De Gruyter, 2023).

Fifield, P., 'Samuel Beckett: Out of the Archive, An Introduction', *Modernism/Modernity*, 18 (2011), 673–9.

Fisher, M., *Scribal Authorship and the Writing of History in Medieval England* (Columbus: Ohio State University Press, 2012).

Garland, R., '*A First Catalogue of Attic Peribolos Tombs*', Annual of the British School at Athens, 77 (1982).

Gay, J., *Polly: An Opera – Being the Second Part of The Beggar's Opera* (London: no. pub., 1729).

Gell, A., *Art and Agency* (Oxford: Clarendon, 1998).

Gitelman, L., *Paper Knowledge: Toward a Media History of Documents* (Durham, NC: Duke University Press, 2014).

Gontarski, S. E., 'Greying the Canon: Beckett and Performance', in S. E. Gontarski and A. Uhlmann, eds., *Beckett after Beckett* (Gainesville: University Press of Florida, 2006), 141–57.

Görke, A., and Hirschler, K., *Manuscript Notes as Documentary Sources* (Beirut: Orient-Institut, 2011).

Greene, R. L., *The Early English Carol*, 2nd ed. (Oxford: Clarendon Press, 1977).

Griffiths, J., 'Unrecorded Middle English Verse in the Library at Holkham Hall, Norfolk', *Medium Aevum*, 64 (1995), 278–84.

Hale, M., *Historia Placitorum Coronae: The History of the Pleas of the Crown*, 2 vols. (London: Nutt and Gosling, 1736).

Hobbins, D., *Authorship and Publicity before Print: Jean Gerson and the Transformation of Late Medieval Learning* (Philadelphia: University of Pennsylvania Press, 2009).

Hordern, J. H., *The Fragments of Timotheus of Miletus* (Oxford: Oxford University Press, 2002).

Hughes, T. P., 'The Evolution of Large Technological Systems', in W. E. Bijker, T. P. Hughes, and T. Pinch, eds., *The Social Construction of Technological Systems* (Cambridge, MA: MIT Press, 2012), 45–76.

Humphreys, S. C., *Kinship in Ancient Athens: An Anthropological Analysis* (Oxford: Oxford University Press, 2019).

Jameson, F., *Postmodernism or, The Cultural Logic of Late Capitalism* (London: Verso, 1989).

Jangchup Gyeltsen, *Rlangs kyi po ti bse ru rgyas pa [“The Rhinoceros Book”; Biography of the Divine Rlang Lineage]*, ed. Tséten Phüntsok (Lhasa: Bod ljong mi dmangs dpe skrun khang, 1986).

Jansen, B., *The Monastery Rules: Buddhist Monastic Organization in Pre-Modern Tibet* (Oakland: University of California Press, 2018).

Jarrahi, M. H., Lutz, C., and Newlands, G., ‘Artificial Intelligence, Human Intelligence and Hybrid Intelligence Based on Mutual Augmentation’, *Big Data and Society*, 9(2) (2022), https://doi.org/10.1177/20539517221142.

Jarvis, J., *The Gutenberg Parenthesis* (New York: Bloomsbury Academic, 2023).

Jikten Gonpo Rinchen Pel, ‘Gdan sa nyams dmas su gyur skabs mdzad pa’i bca’ yig [Monastery rule produced during the deterioration of the monastic seat]’, in *The Collected Works (Bka’ ’bum) of Skyob pa ’Jig rten gsum mgon*, ed. H. H. Drikung Kyabgöon Chetsang, 12 vols. (Delhi: Drikung Kagyu Ratna Shri Sungrab Nyamso Khang, 2001), iv, 126–8.

Johnson, S., *A Dictionary of the English Language* (London: Knapton, 1755).

Johnson, W. A., *Bookrolls and Scribes in Oxyrhynchus* (Toronto: University of Toronto Press, 2004).

Jungherr, A., Rivero, G., and Gayo-Avello, D., *Retooling Politics: How Digital Media Are Shaping Democracy* (Cambridge: Cambridge University Press, 2020).

Jungherr, A., and Schroeder, R., *Digital Transformations of the Public Arena* (Cambridge: Cambridge University Press, 2021).

Kapstein, M., *The Tibetan Assimilation of Buddhism: Conversion, Contestation, and Memory* (Oxford: Oxford University Press, 2000).

‘The Indian Literary Identity in Tibet’, in S. Pollock, ed., *Literary Cultures in History* (Berkeley: University of California Press, 2003), 747–802.

Keesling, K., *The Votive Statues of the Athenian Acropolis* (Cambridge: Cambridge University Press, 2008).

Kinservik, M. J., *Disciplining Satire: The Censorship of Satiric Comedy on the Eighteenth-Century London Stage* (Lewisburg, PA: Bucknell University Press, 2002).

'The Dialectics of Print and Performance after 1737', in J. Swindells and D. F. Taylor, eds., *The Oxford Handbook of the Georgian Theatre 1737–1832* (Oxford: Oxford University Press, 2014), 123–39.

Kleberg, T., 'Commercio librario ed editoria nel mondo antico', in G. Cavallo, *Libri, editori e pubblico nel mondo antico* (Roma: Laterza, 1975).

Kotwick, M. E., *Der Papyrus von Derveni* (Berlin: Walter de Gryuter, 2017).

Krimsti, F., 'Signatures of Authority: Colophons in Seventeenth-Century Melkite Circles in Aleppo', in C. D. Bahl and Stefan Hanß, eds., *Scribal Practice and the Global Cultures of Colophons, 1400–1800* (Basingstoke: Palgrave Macmillan, 2022), 109–32.

Krstić, T., and Terzioğlu, D., *Entangled Confessionalizations? Dialogic Perspectives on the Politics of Piety and Community Building in the Ottoman Empire, 15th–18th Centuries* (Piscataway, NJ: Gorgias Press, 2022).

Lähnemann, H., 'Margarethe von Savoyen in ihren literarischen Beziehungen', *Encomia-Deutsch*, 2 (2002), 159–73.

'From Print to Manuscript: The Case of a Workshop in Stuttgart around 1475', in M. C. Fischer and W. A. Kelly, eds., *The Book in Germany* (Edinburgh: Merchiston, 2010), 17–34.

Lähnemann, H., and Kröner, T., 'Die Überlieferung des Sigenot: Bildkonzeptionen im Vergleich von Handschrift, Wandmalerei und Frühdrucken', *Jahrbuch der Oswald von Wolkenstein-Gesellschaft*, 14 (2004), 175–88.

Lane, E. W., *An Arabic-English Lexicon*, 8 vols. (London: Williams and Norgate, 1863–93).

Lawton, C. L., *Attic Document Reliefs: Art and Politics in Ancient Athens* (Oxford: Clarendon Press, 1995).

Lewis, S. C., and Simon, F. M., 'Why Human-Machine Communication Matters for the Study of Artificial Intelligence in Journalism', in A. L. Guzman, R. McEwen, and S. Jones, eds., *The SAGE Handbook of Human-Machine Communication* (New York: SAGE, 2023), 516–23.

Liddel, P., 'The Places of Publication of Athenian State Decrees from the 5th Century BC to the 3rd Century AD', *Zeitschrift für Papyrologie und Epigraphik*, 143 (2003), 79–93.

Love, H., *Scribal Publication in Seventeenth-Century England* (Oxford: Clarendon Press, 1993).

Mack, W., 'Vox Populi, Vox Deorum? Athenian Document Reliefs and the Theologies of Public Inscription', *Annual of the British School at Athens*, 113 (2018).

McDonald, P. D., 'Calder's Beckett', in M. Nixon, ed., *Publishing Samuel Beckett* (London: British Library, 2011), 153–70.

Menze, V. L., *Justinian and the Making of the Syrian Orthodox Church* (Oxford: Oxford University Press, 2008).

Miller, T., *Late Modernism: Politics, Fiction, and the Arts Between the World Wars* (Berkeley: University of California Press, 1999).

Milmo, D., 'Two US Lawyers Fined for Submitting Fake Court Citations from ChatGPT', *The Guardian*, 23 June 2023.

Mitchell, M., *Artificial Intelligence: A Guide for Thinking Humans* (London: Pelican, 2019).

Morse, D. R., *Radio Empire: The BBC's Eastern Service and the Emergence of the Global Anglophone Novel* (New York: Columbia University Press, 2020).

The Multigraph Collective, *Interacting with Print: Elements of Reading in the Era of Print Saturation* (Chicago: University of Chicago Press, 2018).

Murphy, K. D., and O'Driscoll, S., eds., *Studies in Ephemera: Text and Image in Eighteenth-Century Print* (Lewisburg, PA: Bucknell University Press, 2013).

Murre-van den Berg, H. L., *Scribes and Scriptures: The Church of the East in the Eastern Ottoman Provinces (1500–1850)* (Leuven: Peeters, 2015).

Needham, P., *The Printer and the Pardoner* (Washington, DC: Library of Congress, 1986).

Ní Chroidheáin, A., ed., *Dangerous Creations* (Oxford: Taylor Institution, 2022).

Nielsen, R. K., 'The One Thing Journalism Just Might do for Democracy', *Journalism Studies*, 18 (2017), 1251–62.

Niskanen, S., 'Introduction', in S. Niskanen and V. Rovere, eds., *The Art of Publication from the Ninth to the Sixteenth Century* (Turnhout: Brepols, 2023), 11–22.

North, M., *Reading 1922: A Return to the Scene of the Modern* (Oxford: Oxford University Press, 1999).

Orr, B., 'Theatrical Censorship and Empire', in D. O'Shaughnessy, ed., *The Censorship of Eighteenth-Century Theatre: Playhouses and Prohibition, 1737–1843* (Cambridge: Cambridge University Press, 2023), 95–113.

Osborne, R., *Athens and Athenian Democracy* (Cambridge: Cambridge University Press, 2010).

Osborne, R., and Rhodes, P. J., eds., *Greek Historical Inscriptions: 478–404 BC* (Oxford: Oxford University Press, 2017).

O'Shaughnessy, D., 'Introduction: Theatre Censorship and Georgian Cultural History', in D. O'Shaughnessy, ed., *The Censorship of Eighteenth-Century Theatre: Playhouses and Prohibition, 1737–1843* (Cambridge: Cambridge University Press, 2023), 1–32.

Ott, N. H., 'Die Handschriften-Tradition im 15. Jahrhundert', in B. Tiemann, ed., *Die Buchkultur im 15. und 16. Jahrhundert* (Hamburg: Maximilian-Gesellschaft, 1995), I, 47–124.

Parker, R., *Polytheism and Society in Ancient Athens* (Oxford: Oxford University Press, 2005).

Pasquali, G., *Storia della tradizione e critica del testo* (Firenze, 1934).

Pébarthe, C., *Cité, démocratie et écriture: histoire de l'alphabétisation d'Athènes à l'époque classique* (Paris: De Boccard, 2006).

Pemba, L., *Tibetan Proverbs* (Dharamsala: Library of Tibetan Works and Archives, 1996).

Phillips, A., *Turning the Page: The Evolution of the Book* (London: Routledge, 2014).

Pirie, F., 'Buddhist Law in Early Tibet: The Emergence of an Ideology', *Journal of Law and Religion*, 32 (2017), 406–22.

Pitt, R., 'Just as It Has Been Written: Inscribing Building Contracts at Lebadeia', in N. Papazarkadas, ed., *The Epigraphy and History of Boeotia* (Leiden: Brill, 2014), 373–94.

'Little Epigraphy: Texts on Public and Private Objects', *Lampas*, 54 (2021), 119–36.

Plato, *Cratylus. Parmenides. Greater Hippias. Lesser Hippias*, ed. H. N. Fowler (Cambridge, MA: Harvard University Press, 1926).

Plowden, E., *Les Comentaries, ou les Reportes* (London: Tottell, 1571).

Rabenstein, G., 'Using AI to Predict Shat Should Go Behind a Paywall', *Google*, 2021, https://blog.google/outreach-initiatives/google-news-initiative/using-ai-predict-what-should-be-behind-paywall/ [accessed 15 November 2021].

Pliny the Younger, *Letters*, ed. B. Radice, 2 vols. (Cambridge, MA: Harvard University Press, 1969).

Rainey, L., *Institutions of Modernism: Literary Elites and Public Culture* (New Haven, CN: Yale University Press, 1998).

Raithby, J., ed., *The Statutes of the Realm*, 11 vols. (London: Record Commission, 1819).

Rhodes, P. J., 'Public Documents in the Greek States: Archives and Inscriptions Part I', *Greece and Rome*, 48 (2001), 33–44, 136–53.

Rhodes, P. J., and Osborne, R., eds., *Greek Historical Inscriptions: 404–323 BC* (Oxford: Oxford University Press, 2003).

Rückert, P., Oschema, K., and Thaller, A., *Die Tochter des Papstes: Margarethe von Savoyen* (Stuttgart: Kohlhammer, 2020).

Rudolph, P., 'Buchkunst im Zeitalter des Medienwandels: Die deutschsprachigen Bibelcodices der Henfflin-Werkstatt vor dem Hintergrund der spätmittelalterlichen Ikonographie' (MA thesis, KU Eichstätt-Ingolstadt, 2008).

Rushton Fairclough, H. (trans.), *Horace. Satires. Epistles. The Art of Poetry*. (Cambridge, MA: Harvard University Press, 1926).

Rustow, M., *The Lost Archive: Traces of a Caliphate in a Cairo Synagogue* (Princeton: Princeton University Press, 2020).

Sakya Pandita, *Gsung 'bum (dpe bsdur ma) [Collected Works (critical edition)]*, ed. Dpal brtsegs bod yig dpe rnying zhib 'jug khang, 4 vols (Beijing: Krung go'i bod rig pa dpe skrun khang, 2007).

Schlosser, M., 'Agency', in E. N. Zalta, ed., *The Stanford Encyclopedia of Philosophy* (Stanford, CA: Metaphysics Research Lab, 2019), https://plato.stanford.edu/archives/win2019/entries/agency/ [accessed 18 July 2023].

Schoch, R. W., '"A Supplement to Public Laws": Arthur Murphy, David Garrick, and 'Hamlet, with Alterations"', *Theatre Journal*, 57 (2005), 21–32.

Schwartz, K. A., 'Book history, print, and the Middle East', *History Compass*, 15 (2017), doi: org/10.1111/hic3.12434.

'Did Ottoman Sultans Ban Print?', *Book History*, 20 (2017), 1–39.

Shastri, P. T., *Like a Yeti Catching Marmots* (Boston: Wisdom, 2012).

Shoemaker, P. J., and Reese, S. D., *Mediating the Message in the 21st Century: A Media Sociology Perspective* (New York: Routledge, 2013).

Siegele, L., 'How AI Could Change Computing, Culture and the Course of History', *The Economist*, 20 April 2023.

Simon, F. M., *Artificial Intelligence in the News. How AI Retools, Rationalizes, and Reshapes Journalism and the Public Arena* (New York: Tow Center for Digital Journalism, January 2024), www.cjr.org/tow_center_re ports/artificial-intelligence-in-the-news.php.

Sørensen, P. K., and Erhard, F. X., 'An Inquiry into the Nature of Tibetan Proverbs', *Proverbum*, 30 (2013), 281–309.

Sørensen, P. K., and Hazod, G., *Rulers on the Celestial Plain: Ecclesiastic and Secular Hegemony in Medieval Tibet*, 2 vols. (Vienna: Österreichische Akademie der Wissenschaften, 2007).

Spyra, U., and Effinger, M., 'Schwäbische Werkstatt des Ludwig Henfflin', *Universitätsbibliothek Heidelberg: Bibliotheca Palatina Online*, https:// digi.ub.uni-heidelberg.de/de/bpd/glanzlichter/oberdeutsche/henf flin.html [accessed 5 March 2024].

Stevens, J., and Fallows, D., eds., *Mediaeval Carols*, 3rd ed. (London: Stainer & Bell, 2018).

Stewart, A. F., *Art, Desire and the Body in Ancient Greece* (Cambridge: Cambridge University Press, 1998).

Stieber, M., *The Poetics of Appearance in the Attic Korai* (Austin: University of Texas Press, 2004).

Stock, B., *The Implications of Literacy* (Princeton: Princeton University Press, 1983).

Sullivan, H., 'Why Do Authors Produce Textual Variation on Purpose? Or, Why Publish a Text That Is Still Unfolding?', *Variants*, 12–13 (2016), 77–103.

Svenbro, J., *Phrasikleia: An Anthropology of Reading in Ancient Greece*, trans. J. Lloyd (Ithaca, NY: Cornell University Press, 1993).

Tahkokallio, J., 'Theories, Categories, Configurations', in S. Niskanen and V. Rovere, eds., *The Art of Publication from the Ninth to the Sixteenth Century* (Turnhout: Brepols, 2023), 371–81.

Tamkin, A., Brundage, M., Clark, J., and Ganguli, D., 'Understanding the Capabilities, Limitations, and Societal Impact of Large Language Models', arXiv, 4 February 2021, http://arxiv.org/abs/2102.02503 [accessed 24 February 2021].

Taşğın, A., and Langer, R., 'The Establishment of the Syrian Orthodox Printing Press', in G. Roper, ed., *Historical Aspects of Printing and Publishing in Languages of the Middle East* (Leiden: Brill, 2013), 181–92.

Taylor, M. A., 'Outside Joke: Virginia Woolf's Freshwater and Coterie Insularity', *Modernist Cultures*, 18 (2023), 241–60.

Tether, L., *Publishing the Grail in Medieval and Renaissance France* (Cambridge: Boydell and Brewer, 2017).

'The Digital Index of Medieval English Verse', www.dimev.net.

Thomas, D., 'The 1737 Licensing Act and Its Impact', in J. Swindells and D. F. Taylor, eds., *The Oxford Handbook of the Georgian Theatre 1737–1832* (Oxford: Oxford University Press, 2014), 90–106.

Thomas, R., 'Edmund Plowden', *Notes and Queries*, 270 (1867), 184.

Tite, C. G. C., *The Early Records of Robert Cotton's Library: Formation, Cataloguing, Use* (London: British Library, 2003).

Tracy, S. V., *The Lettering of an Athenian Mason* (Princeton: ASCSA, 1975). *Athenian Lettering of the Fifth Century B.C: The Rise of the Professional Letter Cutter* (Berlin: De Gruyter, 2016).

Trumble, E., *Fauxbourdon: An Historical Survey* (Brooklyn: Institute of Medieval Music, 1959).

Van Hulle, D., 'The Text as Figure and Ground: Beckett and Electronic Publishing', in M. Nixon, ed., *Publishing Samuel Beckett* (London: British Library, 2011), 219–28.

'Introduction: A Beckett Continuum', in D. Van Hulle, ed., *The New Cambridge Companion to Samuel Beckett* (Cambridge: Cambridge University Press, 2015), xvii–xxvi.

'Modern manuscripts', *Oxford Research Encyclopaedia of Literature* (Oxford: Oxford University Press, 2019).

Weller, S., 'Beckett's Last Chance: Les Éditions de Minuit', in M. Nixon, ed., *Publishing Samuel Beckett* (London: British Library, 2011), 113–30.

Wessel, J., *Owning Performance | Performing Ownership: Literary Property and the Eighteenth-Century British Stage* (Ann Arbor: University of Michigan Press, 2022).

Whitley, J., 'Why με? Personhood and agency in the earliest Greek inscriptions', in P. J. Boyes, P. M. Steele, and N. Elvira Astoreca, eds., *The Social and Cultural Contexts of Historic Writing Practices* (Oxford: Oxbow, 2021), ii, 269–87.

von Wilamowitz-Moellendorff, U., *Timotheos, Die Perser* (Leipzig: Hinrichs, 1903).

Winton, C., *John Gay and the London Theatre* (Lexington: University Press of Kentucky, 1993).

Wojahn, D., 'Lama Dampa's Open Letter Promoting Vegetarianism', *Yeshe*, 3(1) (2023), https://yeshe.org/lama-dampas-open-letter-promoting-vegetarianism/ [accessed 18 January 2024].

'Inherited Stories, Timeless Wisdom: Intertextuality and Proverbs in the *Aché Lhamo Namthar*', *Journal of Tibetan Literature*, 3 (2024), 45–70.

Wolfram, S., 'What Is ChatGPT Doing . . . and Why Does It Work?', *Stephen Wolfram*, 2023, https://writings.stephenwolfram.com/2023/02/what-is-chatgpt-doing-and-why-does-it-work/ [accessed 30 May 2023].

Cambridge Elements ⊒

Publishing and Book Culture

SERIES EDITOR
Samantha J. Rayner
University College London

Samantha J. Rayner is Professor of Publishing and Book
Cultures at UCL. She is also Director of UCL's Centre for
Publishing, co-Director of the Bloomsbury CHAPTER
(Communication History, Authorship, Publishing, Textual
Editing and Reading), and co-Chair of the Bookselling
Research Network.

ASSOCIATE EDITOR
Leah Tether
University of Bristol

Leah Tether is Professor of Medieval Literature and Publishing
at the University of Bristol. With an academic background in
medieval French and English literature and a professional
background in trade publishing, Leah has combined her
expertise and developed an international research profile in
book and publishing history from manuscript to digital.

About the Series

This series aims to fill the demand for easily accessible, quality texts available for teaching and research in the diverse and dynamic fields of publishing and book culture. Rigorously researched and peer-reviewed Elements will be published under themes, or 'Gatherings'. These Elements should be the first check point for researchers or students working on that area of publishing and book trade history and practice: we hope that, situated so logically at Cambridge University Press, where academic publishing in the UK began, it will develop to create an unrivalled space where these histories and practices can be investigated and preserved.

Cambridge Elements ⸗

Publishing and Book Culture

Publishing and Book History

Gathering Editor: Andrew Nash

Andrew Nash is Reader in Book History and Director of the
London Rare Books School at the Institute of English Studies,
University of London. He has written books on Scottish and
Victorian Literature, and edited or co-edited numerous
volumes including, most recently, *The Cambridge History of the
Book in Britain, Volume 7* (Cambridge University Press, 2019).

Gathering Editor: Leah Tether

Leah Tether is Professor of Medieval Literature and Publishing
at the University of Bristol. With an academic background in
medieval French and English literature and a professional
background in trade publishing, Leah has combined her
expertise and developed an international research profile in
book and publishing history from manuscript to digital.

Printed in the United States
by Baker & Taylor Publisher Services